There's something magical about looking at business like a game. The business pressures don't change, but the "game" perspective gives permission to view those pressures differently. In *The Best Game*, Michael masterfully marries the dynamics of running a businesses with the way we "play," making them virtually indistinguishable. Such an approach may sound trivial on the surface, but has transformed the way my company operates . . . for the better. The way our team deals with each other, the way the company addresses challenges, the way we celebrate victories, it's all there. Every chapter goes deeper into the game dichotomy with actionable steps to renew corporate culture, bring employees together, and set the stage for success.

Brent Wheelbarger
CEO, Trifecta Communications Co-Founder, Viribus VR Labs

I met Michael Smith twenty years ago. He had a reputation as a wise mentor with a heart to serve young leaders. I've personally benefited from *The Best Game* principles and have witnessed their impact on many other leaders and leadership teams. The principles in this book didn't emerge from academic study but from a lifetime of leading organizations and serving leaders. *The Best Game* is a treasure of wisdom for doers.

Lance Humphreys
CEO, Salt and Light Leadership Training

Not only has *The Best Game* made business fun and

empowering, it also has given me a new perspective on how to live my best life. Its teaching is universally applicable. Every day is a game and my amazing team, and I have a playbook to help us march down the field to our shared successes. As a young leader, one of the greatest gifts I have received has been the training from this book.

Armand McCoy
President, Trifecta Communications

I had the opportunity and honor to work with Michael Smith (or Smitty) and implement the principles laid out in *The Best Game*. Little by little, I eventually transformed the way I approached my business. I only wish it could have happened sooner. In all candor, I was really searching for affirmation, not knowledge. I owned a relatively successful business, and I didn't really think I could learn much more about business and leadership. It is clear to me now that I not only had more to learn, but I needed different perspectives. We all understand the concept of games, and we play them in some facet or another every day. Using this game context with your business makes business easier to approach and understand, and it helps make the everyday challenges more fun. The most rewarding part for me was figuring out my *why*. It was hard to get past money, but as Smitty told me, money is just a by-product of any business, and if that's your *why*, your business probably won't last long. *The Best Game* provides the tools and guidance to develop you into a better leader, thus developing your company into a better business. There are very few things I could recommend with a higher degree of certainty than this book and its strategies!

Lance Morton
Owner, The Morton Group

I love the way Michael Smith (Smitty) talks about leadership and the intentionality he puts into his thoughts. They are grounded in reality and practicality, not just theory. He has helped me and my team over the years. As a leader of a nonprofit, I can wholeheartedly say that his principles apply. All of us ask WIIFM (read the book to find out what that means)! Understanding just this concept, not to mention so many others, will dramatically help you move the ball down the field in your business or nonprofit.

Rodney Huffty
Young Life Area Developer, Cimarron Region

As a competitor, I hate losing. *The Best Game* gave me the secrets and strategies I need to ensure victory in my business. This book and the man who wrote it helped take a small idea and turn it into a movement that has helped to radically change thousands of lives. Without this book, Hope is Alive does not exist. This is a *must* read for every entrepreneur.

Lance Lang
Founder, Hope is Alive Ministries

The Best Game has been a great resource for our organization as we manage rapid growth. The principles are easy to remember and team members have been eager to implement them. The book is laid out in such a way that it can be used with a guide to encourage every member on the team to join the best game. "Your success is directly proportional to the number of difficult conversations you are willing to have" should be tattooed on my hand as a permanent reminder that our organization is best served when I step into the difficult conversations rather than avoid them. This book and the principles included are a great resource that I use time and time again as we bring on new team members and grow our leadership.

Joanna T. Smith
CEO, Executive Director, Hearts for Hearing

The Best Game is essential for anyone who is currently in leadership or plans to lead. Michael Smith's deep understanding of what it takes to be successful is masterfully articulated in the pages of this book. The principles found in the book are essential and pertinent for those of us who lead in businesses, ministries, nonprofits, and life in general. *The Best Game* stands as one of the great playbooks for vision and success.

Nicholas A. Lee
Pastor, The Christ Experience

THE BEST GAME

A SIMPLE AND MEMORABLE MODEL FOR SUCCESSFULLY RUNNING ANY ORGANIZATION

MICHAEL S. SMITH

CONTENTS

Acknowledgments   xiii
Foreword   xvii
Preface   xxi

Introduction   1
GOALS   9
RULES   25
PLAYERS   41
STRATEGY   73
MEASURES   97

Afterword   119

ABOUT GRAY SPARROW BOOKS

Sparrows are the humblest of birds. They represent the common person. We can't all soar like eagles or strut like peacocks.

Gray Sparrow Books seeks to give a voice to the humblest among us who have a message for the world. We think *everyone* should be able to hear from these thought leaders, storytellers, practitioners. We want to share their wisdom so we all can learn and grow.

Here's to these birds, these people, these ideas.

ACKNOWLEDGMENTS

Getting this book published was a lot more work than I expected. I thought the work of writing, revising, and revising again was the bulk of the process, and that once I had done that, I would hold a copy of my book within a month. Little did I know that I had only completed maybe half of the process of publishing a book. Maybe it is better that I didn't know how many revisions and edits and steps to design and publication were still in my future. There are several people who made the whole process more bearable and often even enjoyable.

However I want to especially thank my life partner, Joanna. True to her nature, she has supported me since grade school (really) and was patient many days when my laptop was my too-constant companion as I wrote and rewrote.

Thank you.

For My Dad

He taught me how to work and play.
And often they were the same thing.
For him, there was no obstacle in work or
play that could not be overcome with focus,
perseverance, and creative thinking.

FOREWORD

You know the quotes:

"Get the right people on the bus and in the right seats."
"People aren't primarily motivated by a paycheck."
"Culture wins every time."

I've heard them, too. And I often wondered what they really meant and how to put them into practice to get tangible results. How do I lead better? How do I inspire and encourage people? How do I foster a winning culture? How do I know I have the right people? Over the years, I've read many books on vision, mission, and leadership, and they often come up short. Not that the content isn't excellent, or the lessons aren't real, but I can't take the content and do something useful with it.

My job is President. The company is Computer-Rx. If you haven't heard of us, it doesn't mean you haven't been affected by us. We power community pharmacies across the nation that provide healthcare.

Our company has been around for more than thirty years. While we have a history of success and a recognizable brand in our industry, I think we are still in our infancy and have great opportunity to play a role in changing the health-care industry for the better.

As the leader of the company, I must always ask how we can improve and achieve our goals. I must always seek to get better personally, because if I don't improve the company likely won't improve. While pursuing this journey of personal and professional growth, I was introduced to Michael Smith. I was working for my family's business and looking for leadership advice to help navigate the waters. I knew his story was similar and thought he could provide guidance.

Honestly, when I started the journey with Michael I had no idea what to expect. I just knew I needed help and wanted to grow. Quickly during the process, I realized my leadership was improving drastically, and I was growing in my own self-confidence. Michael led me through the material in this book, and so much began to become clear.

I was searching for my own mission; I just didn't know it. He pressed me to develop my personal *why* statement that translated crafting the *why* for the company. After reading many books on mission, vision, and leadership, I'd never actually developed my own vision much less one for the company.

Through the lessons that follow, I learned more about myself, the value I bring to the table, and my role as leader. When I was midway through the process with Michael, I transitioned to the role of the president and I had the tools to be successful. I believed in my team and knew it was my job to foster a culture, invest in the team, and create a framework for them to be successful. I began to put into practice what I was learning—teaching my leadership team how to lead by example.

The process in this book: Goals, Rules, Players, Strategy, and Scoreboard began to filter into everything we did. Though we are constantly refining our process, the results have been astonishing. We are now going through the process as a leadership team and are creating a leadership development program in order to invest in as many staff members as we can. We understand the importance of investing in our people and believe this model is invaluable to the future of our company.

We are creating passion, clarity, and engaged employees who understand why we exist as a company and what value they bring to the table. We have strengthened our culture and empowered the team to see the part they play in achieving the objectives. We understand what players we need on our team to be successful. We are measuring and rewarding success and having fun. I periodically go back to the book as a reference or read it again as a reminder of the fundamentals. Leadership can be over complicated and overwhelming. However, when you understand the foundation and work within this book, it becomes increasingly simple and success follows. I hope you will play *The Best Game*. It will be an invaluable investment you can make in your business.

Lauren Warkentine

President, Computer-Rx

PREFACE

This Second Edition of *The Best Game* is a revised and edited collection of knowledge and useful tools borne out of over forty years of leadership and mentoring experiences. I hope it will provide you with a framework to both improve your effectiveness as an influencer, as well as make your work in your organization more fun and satisfying. These tools took a young, ambitious man (me) from my first real job to business success, and then eventually to what I do today.

I have the best job I could ever imagine: providing leaders tools that make success a habit. Though I earned English and Education Degrees in college, my first real job was as a production supervisor in a small manufacturing business. I loved it. In many ways, it was like the teaching I was trained to do. I was getting a group of people—mostly working men —to do something they couldn't or wouldn't do on their own.

To succeed, I learned to:

• Define what we wanted to accomplish.

• Determine, and then train for skills to get the jobs done.
• Ensure jobs were done well, on time, and as profitably as possible.

Now I have assembled the principles, tools, and resources that helped me be a successful CEO, and I use them as the foundation to help others make a significant impact in their organizations.

God has blessed me greatly, and I want to be a blessing to others. That is why I want to help you win. To do so, I will use the analogy of how leading an organization is like a game. This will give you a memorable framework as you build your own method to lead and influence others.

I hope the process of learning The Best Game Model of Leadership will serve you well as you grow into the leader you need to be and were meant to be.

INTRODUCTION

"How do you like being the boss?" my dad asked.

I thought for a minute and said, "Pop, it's like riding on a rocket ship. You can't pull over to the side of the road and think about where we should go and how best to get there. The power of momentum is scary and limits my options, but it is also an adrenaline rush. I am the new captain on a long flight, with no training, no experience. And, I love it. And, I am afraid." My dad was the founder and owner of a business that, with some fear and trembling, and not a small amount of inflated self-confidence, I had asked to lead two months before this conversation.

I had recently returned to work at the manufacturing company he had started twenty years earlier. I was equipped with a Bachelor's Degree in English and Education and a Master's Degree in Human Relations. I had about twelve years of middle-management work experience, both at his manufacturing company and at a couple of Fortune 500 companies.

My dad started the company on an idea and some borrowed money and worked hard to build a small, profitable chemical-manufacturing company with thirty employees. He was a classic command-and-control leader who knew that perseverance, creative thinking, and hard work would solve most problems. It had worked for him. Up to a point.

Then, for the first time since the birth of the company, the financial statements showed a loss for the year. My evaluation was a lack of leadership at the top. That's right, I had to tell my father that basically he wasn't doing the right thing, and I could do better. You can imagine how that conversation went. What made it worse was that my dad was the CEO who had just spent the better part of three months going through recovery for alcoholism, and he had named another man president a couple of years earlier. This man was a very capable sales guy who had been with the company a long time.

To make me the new President, my dad had to first accept the idea that I was capable, which was a stretch. He also had to come to grips with firing himself and demoting the guy who was president, and his friend. By the way, the President also had two of his sons working for the company who I had grown up with. What a mess.

I thought I could do a better job than my successful father and the people he had hired to get the company where it was. Being a little overconfident can sometimes be helpful. My dad bought it.

Now I was the boss. I had the title. I had to change things, get people to think and act differently. All previous leadership had been command-and-control. I was a wannabe hippie. I wanted us all to work together for a common goal. I wanted people to think for themselves. I wanted them to own what they did. Previous leadership had provided motivation through a paycheck, some benefits, and the threat of termination. I had to think of a different way to get employees to do more.

The question I needed to answer was: "What's the best way to make work fun, meaningful, *and* profitable?

To find the answer, I looked back at my less-than-stellar athletic career as a tennis player and golfer. I asked myself why I loved to play games I knew I would never be really good at.

In an "aha moment," I thought about approaching work like a game where the team is paid to play and makes more money when the team wins more. Treating business as a game seemed worth a try.

Leading an Organization Is Like a Game

As you work through the information and exercises in this book, I do not make a distinction between not-for-profit and for-profit organizations. In my experience, while the missions may differ, the way they can and should be run is basically the same. After all, unless you are "too big to fail," a category most of us will never have to worry about, you have to bring in at least a dollar more a year than you spend. And by definition, organizations regardless of their taxable status are made up of people. The principles that work in terms of dealing with people work—or they don't work—no matter what kind of organization they choose to be part of.

We typically think of running a business or organization as "work," something we do to earn money to take care of ourselves and our families. Work is rarely expected to be enjoyable. Work is, well, work.

I believe we can change that. We can do better. All of us spend more time working than any other activity in our lives besides sleeping. We are built to work. We need to work. Contributing to something bigger than ourselves gives us meaning and purpose.

Work should and can be fulfilling, meaningful, and even fun. Unfortunately, for many, work is degrading, depressing, and far from fulfilling. That's just wrong.

How can going to work become something we look forward to—at least most of the time? Is there a way to bring dignity to work rather than shame or dread? Can we find a way to look at ourselves as contributors to making something important happen? Can we be proud to say, "I helped build that, do that, or make that possible?" I think we can. Let's reroute our thinking and consider a football game. Every fall, thousands and thousands of people spend a considerable amount of money on season tickets, fan apparel, and mediocre food (not to mention the time and emotional energy it takes) to watch a game that in the expanse of eternity has little lasting value or meaning toward improving the quality of life for the planet.

Yet the US spends a significant amount of media time reporting on sports in every conceivable detail.

The biggest television event year after year is the Super Bowl. What is there about games that makes us give our precious resources of time, money, and talent to just watch something we don't even play in?

What would happen if we took the same principles that

make games so attractive and applied them to work? What would happen if we approached leading an organization as a game? Not a game as in something unimportant and frivolous, but a game that is important, enjoyable, and meaningful.

Interested? It's not a hard model to imagine or to implement.

Humans Like to Play

We are social animals. We have survived because we depend on each other. We depend on each other for emotional support, entertainment, encouragement, and protection. Especially in a modern society, many of our daily necessities (food, clothing, shelter, and of course wireless internet service) require that we rely on others. Immense satisfaction comes from being part of a team that identifies obstacles, develops solutions, strives to implement, and then succeeds.

Your organization is a social organism made up of people who think, strive, and succeed. While it has a life of its own with needs, behaviors, and goals, it also is made up of people who have lives of their own. The function of any capable leader is to match the needs, behaviors, and goals of the organization to those of the people who choose to join.

In this book, we will give attention to building, nurturing, and maintaining a system of play (work) that succeeds daily. People are made not only to work, but to play, and when we give ourselves to a game, we often play so hard we lose ourselves in the game. It can and often does happen that we can lose ourselves in work. This is called being "engaged."

Successful play requires knowing the rules, knowing how to score, developing the skills needed to play well, having a strategy to win, and a way to keep score, which is really feedback on performance. It also requires having a system or method of monitoring the ever-changing field of play so that all resources are optimally focused on winning moment-to-moment.

Games Are About Doing Something Fun

Leading an organization is about seeing a need or want, figuring out how to satisfy that need or want for a target audience, and do so in a way that sets you up to be able to do so again. The same is true in a game. Working hard to add value and get back more than you put into something can be a game, too. And, done well, it's fun. What makes leading an organization the best game in the world is that it never ends, and when done right, it enriches the lives of everyone involved. The customer has a need that gets taken care of, and the business walks away from the transaction with more than it started with. Games and doing business have five critical ingredients in common.

1. Games have **GOALS.** Business has a goal: make money. Business can have other goals, too, but all the enterprises I know of must eventually make money. Even nonprofits must take in more money than they spend, or they cease to exist. That's the essence of the game.

Sure, there are other ways to score goals: improving quality of life, feeding the economy, and providing meaning for those people who choose to be a part of the organization. These goals can and should be considered in addition to financial sustainability and profit.

2. Games have **RULES.** Business and leadership have rules. Some are non-negotiable, like regulations and laws. Leaders get to make up other rules according to the strategic needs of the organization. Leaders often decide how their organizations treat clients and customers, how they take care of employees, and how they make themselves different from the competition. Break the rules, and you may get penalized or possibly forced out of the game. And that's partly what makes business so much fun—agreed-upon rules.

3. Games have **PLAYERS**. Business also has players, and they significantly contribute to winning or losing. Those players are the organization's decision-makers, employees, consumers, suppliers, and even members of the community in which the business exists. Always the most important players in the game are employees, of which the leader is included. These are the people paid to help get the organization across the designated goal line.

Business is all about people. Getting them to buy from you, sell to you, work for you. And because people are predictable only about half the time, you can be sure the game will always be interesting. Games and leadership both require strategy. Both require keeping the objective in mind and thinking creatively about how to achieve the objective using available resources. Both require maximizing strengths and compensating for weak areas.

4. Games have **STRATEGY**. In a game, there are winners and losers. Organizations have winners and losers. Invest your scarce and precious resources well and get rewarded. If you do it poorly or don't respond well to circumstances, even those outside your control, you risk being forced to

stop playing. All these things are what make leading a business or organization so fascinating.

5. All games **MEASURE** performance. Measurement and competition improve products and services. Measurement and competition refine the rules.

Business is The Best Game!

GOALS

Chapter Goal: *Realize the importance of first clearly defining the overarching goal or "the Why" of your organization. This enables your team to intentionally and consistently work toward that foundational goal.*

I am not an athlete.

I would like to be. I try hard. I am better than some, but not near as good as many. I grew up as a tennis player but also played Little League baseball, golf, and some football. Now, I work out regularly. I ride a road bike. I used to play a lot of racquetball. I accept my athletic place on the sideline partly because I have a lot of company. Like me, there are a lot of athletic wannabes out there, and like me, they work at getting better knowing they will never be famous for how they throw a football, hit a baseball, or swing a golf club. They just want to get better. They want to work toward something.

When I became president of my father's company I had Degrees in English and Education, a Master's Degree in

Human Relations, and a modicum of work experience. I was not qualified to be a CEO. I was an executive wannabe. Maybe because of playing all those sports, I instinctively focused on becoming an effective leader the same way I had approached performing as an athlete: figure out what the goal is, watch what really good players do well, practice techniques that work, get feedback, adjust, and get better. Then do it again. And again. And again.

I became president when I asked to lead the company after it had lost money for the first time in its twenty years. I thought I could help turn it around. The question of course was, what was I going to do to change direction?

As the rookie leader, I gathered my newly drafted decision-makers and suggested we decide what we wanted from the enterprise, what were the key objectives we could pursue with single-minded focus? Like wannabe athletes, we instinctively knew we wanted to get better at what we did.

So we chose a few critical objectives that, if accomplished, would be game changers in terms of operating efficiencies and sales volume. In other words, we clarified what a really good score would look like for our business. The process worked!

Over and over again. We discovered that approaching business as a game and defining goals—what we wanted to accomplish—became a terrific model for building a unified team and for running a profitable, fun business.

Playing to Win What?

Every game has a goal—score more than the other player, beat your personal best time, go faster, jump higher, last longer. The clearer the goal can be defined, the better chance you have getting what you want.

Business is no different. Leading an organization is the best game, and like every great game, there must be an agreed-upon, understood goal.

Leadership is the most important factor determining the ultimate success of any and every organization. While the success of any endeavor is dependent on how well scarce and precious resources are invested for their highest and best use in pursuit of a goal, leadership will always be the long-term major factor determining if the organization wins and how often.

Determining a goal that will focus the energies and resources of the organization is the leader's first and most important job. I get to work with many capable leaders who know how to do something well, like being a salesperson, software developer, writer, health care professional, accountant, or pastor.

But they need help getting a group of people like employees or volunteers to do things they might not otherwise do on their own. Always, always, always, the first thing I ask is what is "it" they want to accomplish, why "it" is important, and how "it"is communicated to their teams. If what the leader wants to accomplish is unclear, it will be impossible to communicate to others why they should give their time or money or both. If the leader is not passionate about the objective, the organization is doomed to mediocrity at best and more likely an impending extinction. Passion is contagious. But so is apathy.

You have chosen to be the leader of your organization, and therefore, you are entrusted with a significant amount of valuable resources not the least of which is the future and well-being of the people who chose to follow you and do business with your organization. Your first and most important job is to define the goal—what you and your organization want to accomplish. What will be the focus of all the decision-making and the precious, limited resources entrusted to you? Define your goal with clarity and passion. This is your first and most important job as leader.

Exercise: Why in One Concise, Clear, Call-To-Action Sentence

We often operate as though people only care about What they are buying (I'll capitalize these words because they're so important I want them to stand out for you as concepts). The reality is that people more often buy Why your product or service is being offered. Simon Sinek explains this principle well in his wildly popular TED Talk, "How Great Leaders Inspire Action." He calls the concept The Golden Circle. He says that everything else being equal people will always choose a product, service, or organization based more on an emotional connection than a rational one. Sure, you must offer a competitive service or product and it must meet the needs and wants of the client. But once that is established, the choice is delegated to your client's or customer's unconscious internal conversation about which option best reflects his or her internal values and principles.

Meaning that opens the door to emotion wins. The evidence is all around us. People don't walk into a boutique coffee shop just for a cup of brewed coffee. Almost all of them can get that in their home or office. They go and spend a lot more at a Starbucks or similar establishments to get basically the same product because they, their friends, and business associates feel comfortable and like the atmosphere at the coffee shop. Their emotions come into play in choosing to get their coffee there.

I go to a car repair shop because it is independently owned by a family who knows my name, treats my wife and kids well, and does quality work, even though it is a bit more expensive than the dealership. I choose to give them my business because I like independent business people who work hard at doing business right. An emotional decision? You bet.

With an organization, again all things being equal, people also will choose to give their time and energy to one that best matches their values. Meaning is an incredibly important strategic tool in getting and keeping clients, customers, and employees.

It's foundational to your success as a leader to also create your own personal Why.

You will use this seemingly simple statement to direct your strategic direction and even your day-to-day decision-making. It will keep you on track, focused, and intentional about reaching for important, challenging goals for you and your team.

My disclaimer is that while a Why sounds simple and needs to be as short as possible to aid in clarity and memory, it is usually difficult and challenging to create. It takes time and feedback from trusted sources to write a Why that inspires action.

After you are familiar with the concept that people buy Why over What, you need to make the concept work for your organization. To do this, build your Why in one concise, clear, call-to-action sentence.

This will be your first and most fundamental leadership tool. This is not your usual mission statement that hangs unnoticed on the conference room wall or is buried in the About Us tab on your website. Your Why in one concise, clear, call-to-action sentence, can be used as both a mantra for meaning and as a measuring stick for activity.

To build a Why that inspires action, work through the following exercise (adapted from *StoryBrand* by Donald Miller).

Step 1: Describe the Problem

What's the pain point you help resolve? In this step, identify who you want to engage and the major problem you help them eliminate. Where is life painful or uncomfortable? You can get specific but keep it concise.

Here's an example from a pre-made dinner delivery service:

> *Parents are so busy in the evening with kids' activities and homework that they don't have time to make a healthy dinner. They end up ordering takeout or eating processed stuff from the freezer.*

There's the target, there's the pain. It's clear, it's relatable, it's specific.

Describe the pain point you help resolve:

-

Step 2: What's Your Solution?

What's your unique solution to that pain point? In this step, show how you take that pain away. What's your solution? The key here is to show how your solution is different from other options.

Back to our meal delivery service:

> *I deliver pre-made wholesome frozen dinners at an affordable weekly price—not just a box of ingredients with a recipe.*
> *This service takes away the pain of scrambling to make dinner or ordering take-out instead. And it's different from other meal-delivery services because the meals are already prepared. There's no extra effort involved for our people.*

Describe your unique solution to that pain point? In this step, show how you take that pain away. The key here is to show how your solution is different than other options.

Now, articulate your solution:

-

Step 3: What Is the Reward?

How does life look after the pain is resolved? Eventually, your Why in one concise, clear, and call-to-action sentence needs to describe how life changes as a result of implementing your solution. This is where you get to describe the transformation of what's possible when that pain goes away.

Again, here is our meal delivery service example:

> *With dinner handled, parents can stop stressing about it, relax, and enjoy time with their families.*

There's the transformation—because those who say "yes" to this service aren't only saying "yes" to dinner (that's more of the What). They want that stress-free time around the table with people they love. That's the Why—family.

Here's how I describe the company Donald Miller created, StoryBrand. See if you can spot the three steps:

> *Most business leaders have trouble explaining what they offer. They're too close to it and they fumble their words. So, we have a seven-part framework that helps business leaders clarify their message. When they do, customers engage. It's the fastest way to grow your business.*

Here's example from my most-recent company, DecisionGrid.

> *DecisionGrid handles the critically important organizational details that may not make it to the top of your priority list. We are the perfect partner to help you grow your passion with deep resources of experience and knowledge in bookkeeping and financial stewardship. We've got your back.*

Now describe what life looks like after the pain your product or service has resolved:

-

Step 4: Formulate Your Why *in one clear, concise, call-to-action sentence.*

Consider using as few words as possible, eight or fewer is ideal. The beauty is in the simple form you will use to write your sentence: Verb/Target/Outcome. Starting the statement with an action verb helps remove the problem of most mission statements: they are inward-focused and self-serving. The bulk of mission statements start with "We," referring to the organization. They don't answer the most basic question everyone has: What's In It For Me? (WIIFM. More on this later). If you don't answer that question quickly, the audience turns its attention to something else faster than you can say, "But this is important to us!" The verb picked must show action. This sets the tone for your action-oriented organization, makes the statement more engaging, and primes the reader to look for an object or target of the verb, which will answer the WIIFM question. It makes us look for who or what is going to receive the benefit of the verb's action, and we always personalize who's going to receive the benefit.

The target then is the who or what that receives the verb's action. It forces us to define where we say we will focus our attention. The more specific you can be here, the better. Clearly identifying your target will help you and your team know what to say yes to and what to say no to.

Finally, the outcome communicates the "value added" or what the target gets by being a recipient of your action. It more fully answers the question: What's In It For Me (WIIFM)? Some examples:

- Ship (verb) software (target) that surprises (outcome).
- Make (verb) people's lives (target) awesome (outcome).
- Ship (verb) orders (target) on-time and accurately (outcome).
- Market (verb) company products for our customers' (target) benefit (outcome).
- And my North Star mission statement for mentoring leaders: Leading (verb) leaders (target) to significance (outcome), by example.

Notice how all these statements are <u>actionable</u> and lead to some sort of measurement and thus, <u>accountability</u>. They make decision-makers think through what they are about, why they do what they do, and what the value is in what they are doing. Writing your organization's Why in one concise, clear, call-to-action sentence can help you do the same.

Choose the most important words in your short paragraph developed in Step 3 making sure that you have at least one in each of the following categories: Verb/Target/Outcome. Then wordsmith the sentence until you have something you can believe in, be proud of, and promote.

<u>Your</u> Why in one short, clear sentence:

-

Engage Your Team: Future Facts

If you don't know where you are going, that's exactly where you will end up. That's not a statement you want to hear from your commercial airline pilot! No coach without a clear vision for his season is going to take his team to the National Championship.

Likewise, organizational leaders and influencers must have clear goals and directions, or else they'll flounder, crash, or lose.

Sadly, most organizations don't know where they are going. So they end up no place in particular and are often mediocre at best.

It is easy for me to check my email immediately when I arrive at my office. I often end the day the same way I started, answering emails, responding to requests from other people. The day ends, and I say to myself, "Wow, I was busy, but what important stuff did I get done?"

There is a big difference between being busy and being fruitful.

Busy means my schedule is full, and I am doing something most of the day. Fruitful means I was busy doing something meaningful and important that got me a little closer to my Why. To get closer to what I want, I first must define what I want, my objective.

After I define my Why, I can better evaluate and focus all opportunities to invest precious and finite resources of time, energy, passion, and money to get something meaningful accomplished. I can stop settling for busyness and instead take intentional steps toward being fruitful and creating the organization I have said is my goal.

You need to have a clear vision of the future you would like to see for your organization. Then you can do the hard work of saying no to requests that don't have enough to do with accomplishing the important. You can choose fruitfulness over mere busyness.

Your Why *in a concise, clear, call-to-action sentence* sets the big-picture objective for your organization. It is the foundation for all of the organization's decision-making and activity. What's next?

You and the team will do your best to build capability and capacity to respond to an envisioned future we will call Future Facts. Your Future Facts will become the organization's vision, which in turn will produce exciting goals.

What Are Future Facts?

> Every sustained success enjoyed by an effective leader and his or her organization derives from a clearly articulated vision. — Robert Steven Kaplan, *What to Ask the Person in the Mirror*.

Can you run your organization without Future Facts? Probably. Many companies do. But efforts and energies invested by teams without Future Facts are more likely to return mixed results at best. Without a clear statement about what your organization will rally around in the day-to-day operation of your business, you are destined to simply react to the hottest circumstance of the moment in the most expedient way. That is a tough business strategy to develop and replicate.

Your team needs a clear picture of what success looks like. As the leader, you need to articulate your organization's vision in tangible form by describing Future Facts.

A good set of Future Facts vividly describes how your organization performs on its best day. They also are your unique blueprint for effectively running the organization. They put a little more flesh on your Why *in a concise, clear, call-to-action sentence*. They also paint a clear picture of where your organization is going. The benefits of powerful Future Facts are that they:

- Show how the organization chooses to spend its valuable and limited resources.
- Motivate your team to accomplish meaningful tasks.

- Act like a compass, always guiding the organization in the right direction.
- Provide inspiration, which is one of the key characteristics people want in their leaders.

Future Facts are <u>positive statements</u> with present tense verbs that describe <u>in detail what really good performance</u> would look like on <u>some fictional day in the future</u>, like by the end of this next year, if everything was working in your favor. To build effective Future Facts lets focus on some of the key phrases in the above definition to get a better understanding.

- <u>Positive statements</u> - Future Facts are about developing a shared sense of destiny. They are about what the group or organization or community members collectively desire. Future Facts aren't about just what the leader wants. To be effective, they have to be about what we all want.
- <u>Really good performance</u> - Future Facts are based on hopes, dreams, and aspirations. They're about exciting possibilities. They're about making a difference, creating something grand, and achieving a new standard of excellence. They tell us the specific, ennobling purpose and greater good we are seeking.
- <u>Some fictional day in the future</u> - Future Facts are a description of an exciting possibility we desire in the future. If it were a description of what existed today, it wouldn't be a Future Fact. It would be an assessment of today's reality. Future Facts are projections. The horizons of Future Facts vary, but generally speaking, five to ten years is a reasonable time horizon.

- If everything were working in your favor - Future Facts stretch our minds out into the future and ask us to dream. Leaders must be able to describe perfect circumstances before they can be realized. By thinking without regard to current reality, leaders encourage others to imagine possibilities and how to achieve them to get there.

Exercise: Build Your Own Future Facts

To build your own Future Facts, make a fictional list of everything that will happen in your organization if you and others are working on your Why in a concise, clear, call-to-action sentence extraordinarily well. Write optimistic facts that reflect what is happening sometime in the future, on your organization's best day, as if you are leading and making happen what you want.

Don't confine your thinking to what is currently happening or what might be accomplished. Instead, paint a word picture of what incredible performance will look like if your Why in a concise, clear, call-to-action sentence is happening without fail.

Take your time. Work a little. Let it sit and then come back to your list. Get input from people who understand and are supportive of what you are trying to do. Edit the Future Facts until they clearly describe what you want your organization to look like on its best day. Check your Future Facts to be sure they are statements that can be measured.

Keep in mind, while your Future Facts are very important, they are not written in stone. They can and most likely will change as your organization matures and grows. Therefore, it is good to plan for periodic review of your list to see whether the objectives you have been working toward have or need to change.

Here are some Future Facts examples:

- *My clients are implementing tools that measurably improve their performance.*
- *Our team measures its success not only by the work that we produce, but also by how our customers use our software. We measure everything within our software to know that we're solving our customer's problems.*
- *Every child feels loved by our staff, and we have personally communicated with parents their children's accomplishments once a week.*
- *We had a record year of growth! The group excelled in teamwork and our spirit is at an all-time high.*

Now it's your turn to work on Future Facts in the four key areas that determine long-term success (for more information on these four critical areas, read Chapter 4).

Your **Customers/Clients Future** Facts:

-

Your **Team** Future Facts:

-

Your **Financial** Future Facts:

-

Your **System** Future Facts:

-

Chapter Takeaways:

1. Just like a game, every organization should have a clear **Goal/Why** that answers, "Why does the organization exist?" And, "What are we trying to accomplish?" Answering the question of Why is fundamental to success.

2. As the leader, you must clearly define why your organization exists. Your Why *in a concise, clear, call-to-action sentence* is your most important leadership tool.

3. To clarify where you want to go and what you want to accomplish, create Future Facts for your organization that describe what accomplishing your Why in a concise, clear, call-to-action sentence would look like on your very best day.

RULES

Chapter Goal: *Share convincingly that the quality of any game, or how any organization is run, is determined by the quality of the Rules you as the leader create. Your Rules determine how you accomplish your Why. You as the leader get to, and must, make the Rules that define how you and your team will treat customers and each other.*

Growing up, I was on the small side. The only real advantage I had was that I was fast. My high school tennis skills were mediocre at best, but what I lacked in form and strategy, I tried to make up for with quick reaction time, hustle, and surprise. For better or worse, I made use of those same characteristics when I became a leader of an organization. I have no doubt that part of my success was due to taking advantage of situations early and quickly, and working hard toward a positive outcome.

On the other hand, learned impetuousness sometimes cost me financially because of my tendency to quick decision-making without all the facts. It also sometimes resulted in pain for the people who worked with me as they had to fix things in the wake of my leadership style. When I assumed the role of President of the manufacturing company, I knew most of the people who worked for me were smarter at what they were doing than I ever could be. I figured if I could create an environment in which they used their strengths for the mission of the organization, we all would win.

I said repeatedly that we were going to do things differently to get different results. I said repeatedly that we were here to make money and have fun. I said repeatedly that our success as an organization depended on the successful nurturing, application, and encouragement of the incredible people who had chosen to work for us. I said repeatedly that while we get to make up a lot of the rules for this business game, as a team we must agree that we will all abide by those rules and that we are all in for the same goal line. I said repeatedly that if we do all the above, the organization would share the fruits of its success.

It worked.

A Game Without Rules Is Not a Game

For a game to work, there must be agreed-upon rules. The clearer the rules, the more the players can focus on strategies to make the best use of operating within those rules and the more creative they can be with their resources. If you as the leader don't make the rules, someone else will. A game without rules is a vacuum waiting to be filled. If you don't fill the vacuum intentionally, other people's rules will leak in and eventually fill all the space, leaving no room for your purposefully chosen, strategically sound rules.

Create less stress for yourself and others by deliberately filling the vacuum early with the rules you choose.

Think of trying to develop a meaningful and productive relationship with someone. If you don't have an intentional conversation about expectations for how the relationship will be meaningful and productive, the vacuum left by avoiding a discussion can be filled with unwanted and unintentional roadblocks. Anger and frustration are more likely to occur.

Being human means we get to choose whether to react to what happens to us or "pro-act" (my word) and have a say in what happens to us. Be proactive. Know that all of us only get one of two things: what we make happen or what we let happen. Decide what you want and then build a few simple, straightforward rules that reflect your values and get you what you want.

Make something cool and important happen.

Discover the Foundation for Your Rules—Build a Values Timeline

> Before you tell your life what you intend to do with it, listen for what it intends to do with you. Before you tell your life what truths and values you have decided to live up to, let your life tell you what truths you embody, what values you represent. — Parker Palmer, *Let Your Life Speak*

Values matter!

Although unseen and intangible, a handful of core values govern our decisions, attitudes, and behavior in life. They permeate everything we do. Our values are shaped by a variety of family, cultural, and peer influences, as well as by life experiences.

Our values are deep-seated, enduring convictions and assumptions that certain attitudes and behaviors are more desirable and preferred than others. They are central to our motivations because they represent deep longings and beliefs about what is best for us.

Personal fulfillment in life and career is directly related to how closely core personal values are lived out. When values are violated by us or are violated by others, some form of strong inner—dissonance and frustration results.

So how do we discover or identify our critically important values, those principles by which we want to live?

The first step is to look back over our lives and identify those important events, both positive and negative, that have shaped our character.

Exercise: Build a Values Timeline

To do that, build a Values Timeline:

> 1. Draw a long, horizontal line across a legal-sized sheet paper. It should begin with your birth date at the left and end with today's date on the far right.
> 2. Below the beginning of the line, write the words "I was born" and your birthdate.
> 3. Below the end point of the line simply write "Today" and today's date.
> 4. Start adding dates and events below the line that you remember as important. Be sure to include the memorable accomplishments and the positive expe-

riences, as well as those that negatively impacted you, your painful experiences. Our life and character are shaped by both.

Some idea starters:

- Graduations from Schools, Degrees Achieved
- Marriage(s) and Divorce(s) (including your parents)
- Birth(s) of Children
- Religious Experiences
- Deaths/Losses of Friendships
- Public Recognitions and Achievements
- Personal Revelations

Take your time putting the Values Timeline together. Let it sit for a period. Go back to it and add events that come to mind.

Once you are satisfied that your timeline is reasonably complete:

1. In the space above the line, write out what you learned from the experience. Describe the value that was formed because of what happened.
2. For instance, if one of your life events was the death of a loved one, a value you might take away from that experience could to "never leave unfinished business with the people you love."
3. If you have a religious experience on your timeline, a value you might take away from that experience could be "nothing happens by accident —God is good, life is good, and I am thankful in all circumstances."

4. Next, review the values you have identified and look for patterns and repetitions. On a separate sheet of paper, transfer all the values you have identified that strike you as principles by which you can live and die. Choose the three or four that are most important to you and give them a one or two-word title and the best definition you can. The idea is to name each value that you identify and then give it words that will clearly communicate what that Value means to you.

Once you are finished, congratulations! You have just identified the most important of your Values.

This is not a finished list. It is dynamic, which means it can and most likely will change as you experience and learn more. Come back to it often, edit it, and add new factors to the list as you discover more things that are important to how you want to live. Just remember to keep the list as short as possible. Too many rules will make you, and those with whom you come into contact, cranky.

Record your Values and give each one some words to help you know what they mean and how they influence your decision-making.

Exercise: Now, From Your Values Write Your Rules

To be successful for the long-term, you and your organization must define the important, consistent behaviors that define your organization. To accomplish that, put together a strategically effective set of Rules for your game. These will guide how you and your team are going to make your Why, your reality. In the context of *The Best Game*, your Rules are those few and critically important behaviors that are not negotiable and define your organization.

As the leader you get to—and you must—make the rules for the game you want your organization to play. You must make the rules because if you don't, someone else will.

Your Rules are written statements that publicly describe behaviors and beliefs that are strategically critical to your organization's success. Rules are magical and effective when done well. They paint a vision of possibility, stir hope, and inspire change.

Almost all leaders make the mistake of thinking the people they lead, and the ones with whom they do business, think like they do. Please don't assume everyone you hire or do business with plays by the same rules you do. They don't. And they won't, unless you intentionally create an environment that demonstrates the understood, established Rules are critical to both individual and organizational success.

As the leader, you have the important responsibility of not only establishing how you want your team to perform, but you also must build ways to enforce the Rules by both positive means such as recognition and celebration as well as negative which may include training, counseling, and even termination.

Your organization's Rules are that important. Rules are:

- Inevitably tied to the leader's convictions and assumptions. *Note: If you haven't completed your Values Timeline, please do that now.*
- About what is best for the organization and its stakeholders.
- Important beliefs and resulting behaviors.

• Strategic. They define how you are going to make your Why happen.
• They are non-negotiable. If they are negotiable, they are not Rules.
• Short. No more than six, but it's better to have four.
• Clear. There is no confusion as to meaning. Explain until everyone understands and can tell anyone at any time.

Starting with the values you identified from your Values Timeline, build the first Rule that is important to making your Why happen. If you could make only one Rule everyone on your team had to follow, no exceptions, what would it be?

Review your Values Timeline again and mold two or three of the Values you identified for yourself into strategic Rules that will differentiate your organization from the competition and, when consistently repeated, will develop loyal clients and contribute to profitability. Draft them:

Now that you have built a strong leadership foundation, let's address how to best influence others to do important things they might not otherwise do on their own.

Engage Your Team: BAM

Running an organization or being responsible for a team can be stressful. Effective leadership reduces the pain and tension that are inevitable when a group of people get together. But instead of being a burden requiring years of training an experience, leadership can be simple. Coach Vince Lombardi promoted the philosophy of becoming "an expert in the basics." That same ideal can make you and your team champions. Leadership can be satisfying rather than stressful. Really.

There is a well-accepted psychological foundation upon which you can build your leadership on:

Everyone Works for Belonging, Affirmation, and Meaning (BAM).

To make your culture and leadership a competitive weapon, think a moment about basic psychology and Abraham Maslow's famous Hierarchy of Needs. His model explains normal human behavior and gives some simple and practical tools for leadership. I'll refresh your memory on the high points of Maslow's Hierarchy of Needs using the following bullet points.

- We are motivated to action based on satisfying our "needs" in a hierarchy of targets.
- The needs at the bottom of the hierarchy must be satisfied before people are motivated to act at the next level.
- Once a need is satisfied it is no longer a motivator.
- As our needs are satisfied, we will move up the hierarchy until we experience the loss of satisfaction at a lower level.
- We will go back to that lower level until our dominant need is satisfied and then start working our way up the pyramid again.
- The first level of need refers to physical needs, such as air, water, and food. The idea is that if we are starving or thirsty, we can only focus on getting food or water.
- Once full, we can concentrate on the next level,

safety. This level of need is all about feeling secure and safe from the possible craziness of the world around us. Having a roof over our heads, a competent and fair police force, and just laws are all safety issues.

• In our culture, physical needs are satisfied by the companies we work for when we get an adequate paycheck that allows us to buy things that satisfy our basic needs.

• Safety needs also are normally taken care of by our employers when they supply a safe working environment and benefits like health and disability insurance and unemployment compensation.

• Remember, however, once a need is taken care of it is no longer a motivator.

So theoretically, if we have our two most basic needs taken care of by our organization, what motivates us? On to the next three levels of the pyramid. Let's make it simple and memorable, and I will offer a slight simplification of Maslow's original hierarchy.

After our tummies are satisfied (or we receive an adequate paycheck) and we feel secure (reasonable benefits and a safe work environment), there are only three things people want: Belonging, Affirmation, and Meaning (BAM), the next three levels on the pyramid of needs.

What this means for leaders is straightforward but profound. Leaders who make a positive difference in the lives of their employees, their clients and customers, and the communities they serve generate dynamic results by building:

Belonging

Creating opportunities for our people to feel part of something bigger than themselves.

Affirmation
Seeking instances where team members' contributions are recognized.

Meaning
Ensuring that what we are doing has significance to connect to hearts and minds.

Everyone works for: Belonging, Affirmation, and Meaning (BAM). This reality should be kept in mind constantly as you are setting the rules that will guide your organization.

Exercise: BAM Self-Assessment

Before you figure out how to incorporate the undergirding reality of BAM into your organization's rules, you can assess your current culture of BAM.

To complete a BAM Self-Assessment, select the number below that most reflects your agreement (ten is the most) or disagreement (one is the least) with the statement for your immediate team.

Belonging
Effective leaders intentionally develop an environment where members feel they are known and part of the team.

1. I know a great deal about my team members' backgrounds, interests, and families, etc.
1 2 3 4 5 6 7 8 9 10

2. I understand what's important to each member of my team.

1 2 3 4 5 6 7 8 9 10

3. I invest in the development of the skills and knowledge of my team.

1 2 3 4 5 6 7 8 9 10

4. I work hard to make team members feel connected to and an important part of the organization.

1 2 3 4 5 6 7 8 9 10

5. There is a climate of openness, respect, and trust among the team.

1 2 3 4 5 6 7 8 9 10

6. Team members have a sense of unity and pride for the team and their work.

1 2 3 4 5 6 7 8 9 10

Affirmation

Effective leaders identify specific behaviors or characteristics in others that contribute to the well-being and mission of the organization, with the end goal of getting those behaviors repeated.

1. When having a conversation with one of my team members, I really listen.

1 2 3 4 5 6 7 8 9 10

2. I regularly praise the work of my team members.

1 2 3 4 5 6 7 8 9 10

3. I regularly give specific feedback, both positive and negative, about any and every team member's performance.
1 2 3 4 5 6 7 8 9 10

4. When I affirm others, it is specific and describes why the work or specific actions were beneficial.
1 2 3 4 5 6 7 8 9 10

5. I am available for guidance and assistance whenever team members need it.
1 2 3 4 5 6 7 8 9 10

Meaning
Effective leaders communicate the end purpose or significance of any and every activity of their organization as it relates to the well-being and mission of the organization.

1. I share with my team members how assigned work is important to the success of the organization.
1 2 3 4 5 6 7 8 9 10

2. If I asked any team member what is important to the organization, I would get pretty much the same answer from everyone.
1 2 3 4 5 6 7 8 9 10

3. I consciously and intentionally set the example for always learning, always getting better.
1 2 3 4 5 6 7 8 9 10

You probably don't need a calculator or a spreadsheet to figure out what you can do better to improve your BAM quotient. Look at your scores in terms of what you think your team needs most. Continue to do those things on which you grade yourself high. In fact, try to get better at them. Look at a couple of middle-of-the-road scores and commit to moving them up at least a couple of notches. If you improve in your good areas, my experience is that the weaker areas will improve as well.

BAM Action Plan

Based on a review of your responses to the BAM Self-Assessment, make a list of the things that you can do to improve the sense of Belonging on your team. What kinds of things can you *do* to Affirm others for activities and behaviors you want repeated? Put together a list of ways you can create and communicate Meaning for your team members.

Using the BAM principle always helps you answer the question every employee and customer is asking: "What's In It For Me?" (WIIFM).

Everyone Wants to Know What's in It for Me?

What's In It For Me (WIIFM) is a life principle that, when understood and correctly applied, not only can make you a more effective leader and influencer, but it will help simplify all your relationships. WIIFM is the question each person asks and answers in every waking moment of every day.

You answered it this morning when your alarm went off. You had choices: You could have turned the alarm off and gone back to sleep. Or you could have silenced the alarm and gotten ready for the day. In either case, you had to determine what was in it for you. If you had chosen to sleep in, you would have been faced with the consequences of that decision. On the other hand, if you had turned off the alarm and gotten out of bed, you decided it was best for you to get moving, unconsciously deciding your day's WIIFM.

In every situation, we make decisions based on our self-interests, or more specifically, on what's most important to creating and maintaining our sense of who we are and who we want to be at that time (it can change). You may be saying to yourself that the proposition sounds egotistical, self-serving, and possibly even dangerous. You are right! The good news is that our Creator enables people to sometimes act unselfishly.

The question is not whether we ask WIIFM. It's how we answer it. As leaders and influencers, however, knowing our audience and having an answer that satisfies the need at hand will determine your success in making good things happen.

Chapter Takeaways:

1. The quality of any game or enterprise is determined by the rules leaders must establish and enforce.

2. Once you pay a livable wage and offer reasonable benefits, encourage great performance using Belonging, Affirmation, and Meaning (BAM).

3. Your job as the leader is to always answer the "What's In It For Me" (WIIFM) question for all stakeholders.

PLAYERS

Chapter Goal: *Communicate that building trust-based relationships with those who choose to follow you or use your services is essential to effective leadership. You must understand that any organizational change must start with you, the leader.*

My midsize chemical manufacturing company was growing. We were making money and having fun. We had acquired a couple of businesses that fit our strategy in different states to expand our markets. As the CEO, I seemed either to be traveling to meet customers and talk to employees, or spending time in my office thinking up the next big thing.

Then we had a fire in our manufacturing plant.

For us, fire was truly a four-letter word, the word we did not want to speak, because in our chemical batching plant all our products were highly flammable. A simple static electricity spark could start a fire that would not just radically harm our business, but also could seriously hurt people. We had a full-time safety staff whose main job was preventative auditing and training. We even had fire drills once a month.

But it happened. It was summer, hot and dry. A static electricity spark from falling liquid lit a mixing tub on fire. The employees responded well but were unable to put out the fire immediately, which meant that in less than 30 seconds we had to evacuate the plant.

The whole team of almost one hundred employees stood outside in the parking lot fearing we might be in deep trouble as smoke poured out the vents in the ceiling. Then the sprinkler system did its job, and the fire was put out. Good news. Really good news.

Which was followed by the bad news. The whole manufacturing area was flooded with water. Most all the tubs had water and in-process product in them, rendering them hazardous waste. Everyone, including me in dress shoes and slacks, began the long, tedious task of cleaning up. We worked side by side in heat and humidity until 6 p.m. when we ordered a truckload of pizzas and pop. Sweaty and dirty, we relaxed for a while, telling and retelling stories of what went wrong, how to ensure it didn't happen again, and how everyone reacted well and bravely. Then we went back to work cleaning up until we were confident we would be back in full production the next day.

As the leader, I made a habit of asking random team members what they liked most about working for our organization, what they liked least, and what they would change. While the answers were almost always helpful, I was continually impressed by how, even years later, employees would remember how all the executives and office staff worked side by side with the rest of the team so the plant would stay open, operating, and on schedule.

Actions speak louder than words when it comes to proving you can be trusted to fully engage as a team member to see the enterprise succeed.

Business Is About People

Most of the leaders I work with were not educated to be leaders. They did not graduate from college with undergraduate or graduate degrees in how to lead an organization. Yes, there are schools that offer such educations, but most of the people I know who end up being the CEO of an organization got there because they did something well. They might have been an inquisitive engineer, an ambitious software coder, a terrific sales person, or like me, a college English major who enjoyed problem-solving and getting stuff done. Many of us find ourselves leading a group of people who are looking to us to set the agenda, to paint a picture of what needs to be done, and to help them know what part they can play to get it done. And because often we have done the work, we can tell others what to do, how to do it, and even when to do it.

That works for a while, and the organization grows because you have a good idea, a good product or service, and you are passionate about it. You enjoy being the boss, bringing something out of the ground, or taking an existing business and giving it life. Then one day cracks begin to appear in the dam. Little ones but leaks nonetheless. There are more and more moments that are not quite so much fun when it comes to running the business. You agree with some of the other CEOs and presidents you hang out with that people are a hassle and if only you didn't have people problems, work would be enjoyable.

You always will be able to trace your organization's problems—product, finance, delivery, manufacturing, and sales —back to people. Often even mechanical problems are a result of people problems; someone either didn't do something he was supposed to or didn't know she was supposed to do something.

If you don't want to deal with people, sell your company ASAP or hire a CEO. Become an employee and submit yourself to someone else's leadership. The people problems won't change. God has a sense of humor. He made people the way they are. You can only work with what you are given. You must get at least as good at leading, managing, and reading people as you were at whatever talent it was that got you to be the boss in the first place. Your new job is to be a psychologist, counselor, cheerleader, judge-jury-executioner, strategist, communicator, and coach *before* you even think about doing what it was that got you into your leadership role in the first place. Really.

I am convinced the only way anyone effectively leads others is through building trust-based relationships with the people who have chosen to follow you. And trust-based relationships are not built overnight or without a lot of work. A lot of work. And time. Work and time. Two commodities of which almost all of us have limited amounts.

And maybe now you know why there aren't many good leaders. There are very few leaders who make building relationships one of their top job duties. On the other hand, my experience is that the amount of energy and time you put into developing trust-based relationships will translate into effectiveness as a leader.

Your most important relationships are with your executive decision-making team. You should be able to trust them completely. If not, fire fast. Your executive decision-makers are the team into which you pour most of your relationship-building energies. They should have the Why of the organization tattooed on the inside of their eyelids.

And it is your executive team who is responsible for driving the Why, the how (Rules), and the what (Future Facts) of your organization down to those who do the work and who buy your services and products. The second level of relationship-building focus must be on your team who reports to your executives. They are significantly influenced by a word or touch from you. You have probably heard in textbooks the management technique called MBWA, "Management by Walking Around." No one leads or manages by simply walking around, but walking around and talking to people about what's important to them and to you will help make you a better leader.

Talking to the people doing the work gives you the chance to hear what works and doesn't in your organization, as well the opportunity and platform to share your passion and vision articulated in your Why, Rules, and Future Facts.

The last group of people you should be spending relationship-building time on is your clients. I do not mean that you shouldn't spend any time on this group—a good leader stays in touch with his constituents—but my experience is that if you spend most of your relationship-building energy on your team members, your clients and customers will not need to hear the message from you because they will be getting it from your employees.

Your Team Is a Direct Reflection of You

If you want to characterize any organization, you don't need to visit its offices. You don't need to look up the organization on the internet. All you really need to do is get to know the leader. The culture of every organization reflects what the leader thinks is important or not important. Everyone in your organization looks to the leader to decide what acceptable behavior and performance looks like.

If your organization is dysfunctional, you most likely don't want it to be that way. But if dysfunction is there, it is because you allow it to go on. You may have lots of rational reasons for allowing it to go on. You may blame it on your employees or something else. But ultimately, if it is there, it is because you as the leader have either consciously or unconsciously let it happen.

On the other hand, if your organization runs like a well-oiled machine, it isn't because it just happened that way. You selected the people, worked on and implemented a repeatable business model, and stayed on top of critical activities to ensure the outputs were relevant to the inputs. What's important to the organization is important to you. Your organization is a direct reflection of you.

So if you want something different for your organization, change yourself first. Organizations don't change bottom-up. They change top-down. That's good news for implementing change, because the variables are limited to one person: you.

As a leader, you must steward your people resources well. And the first person you must steward well is you. If you think of yourself as the organization's most important asset —and you should—then you have a responsibility to manage your limited resources of time, knowledge, energy, passion, skills, abilities, and talents to best serve the organization. You need to manage your own finite resources well, so you can best fulfill your primary leadership role of getting important things done through and with people who wouldn't do them without your direction and influence.

It is the leader's job to make sure the right things get done, the right way, at the right time, by the right people, at the right cost, to achieve the Why of the organization. You want to be fruitful with your resources and work on the business, not just in the business. Working in the business means being busy all day either doing unimportant things or doing important things that could and should be done by someone else. Working on the business means doing the important and necessary things only you as the leader can do.

A suggested to-do list for working on your business would be to:

- Facilitate the creation, ongoing communication, implementation, and monitoring of the organization's Why, Rules, Player Expectations, Strategy, and Results
- Guide, nurture, direct, and evaluate the acquisition and performance of all employees, but especially your executive decision-makers.
- Regularly direct, evaluate, and communicate the success of the organization by establishing and reviewing real-time benchmarks vs. performance and financial statements. This shows progress and status in attaining objectives. When necessary, revise objectives and plans.
- Facilitate the development and implementation of

systems, i.e., the company operational procedures, policies, and standards.

- Maintain awareness of opportunities for expansion, additional customers, new markets, new industry developments, and standards.
- Represent the organization in civic and professional association responsibilities and activities at the local, state, and at the national level. (Other executive leaders bear responsibility for these ventures as interested or assigned as well.)

Leadership requires you to admit you are not capable of doing everything well. It's humbling. Therefore, you must have other capable and committed people available to make important things happen and steward your own resources. In addition, you must be diligent to preserve time to work on the things that only you as the leader can.

No Organization Performs Better Than Its Leader

You are the lid for your organization. You are the constraint to growth, profitability, and success.

Your organization will never accomplish more than you as the leader enable it to accomplish. It will not perform better than you perform. It will not learn better than you learn. You are the choke point. Name one organization that is stronger than its leader. I can't think of one. Even countries and international organizations are direct reflections of the person who leads them. If the leader is innovative, a thoughtful risk-taker, and places high value on people, so does the organization. If the leader is thin on morals and high on greed, so goes the organization. If the leader is the choke point for the growth of the organization, how does the organization grow? The leader must grow.

Jim Collins says in *Good to Great* that there are only two characteristics common to good leaders. The first is personal will. An effective leader knows where the organization is going, how it's going to get there, and it settles for nothing less.

The second common characteristic is humility. A good leader recognizes he or she does not have all the answers, all the energy, or all the tools necessary to make the organization successful.

Therefore, in addition to having other capable people around, a good leader always looks for how he or she can grow. A good leader grows before the organization grows, acts before the organization acts, and changes before the organization changes. How else can a leader show the way and lead? You must lead yourself first. You should ask on a regular basis: Why would someone follow me? How would I answer someone who asks: What's In It For Me?

It's rare for anyone to verbalize the WIIFM question, but you can bet it's always there. And you are always giving some sort of answer to the question, whether spoken or not. In fact, the answers are much more impactful and long-lasting when they are demonstrated by your actions. You cannot lead with your spit-damp finger in the air trying to figure out which way the wind is blowing. Many people can see insincerity from a long way off and won't find attractive a style of leadership built on such an unstable foundation.

Instead, be intentional in leading the organization. If you are going to ask people to follow you, then lead. And lead from your strengths.

Leading from your strengths assumes you know what your strengths are, and yet most of the leaders I know are so busy doing what they are passionate about that they don't take time to do this important work. If you agree with me that success is determined by how well your scarce resources are invested for their best use in pursuit of a goal, then spending the time and energy to understand exactly what you do well and not so well is an invaluable exercise. There are lots of ways to begin that journey and what follows is a pretty good start.

Exercise: Best Self Portrait

Based on an exercise by Robert Quinn, Jane Dutton, and Gretchen Spreitzer from The University of Michigan Ross School of Business, the purpose of this exercise is to help you grow as a leader both in your areas of strength and areas of weakness. First, you will gather feedback from people who know you well and have opinions about who you are when you are at your best. Then you will use the feedback to build a portrait of your best self. Developing this portrait provides insight into the way you add value and make contributions in your organization and other groups.

Begin by identifying three to six people who know you well. They could be colleagues (past or present), friends, family members, or customers. You want to get honest feedback, so think of individuals who will give feedback that is truthful and helpful, not what they think you want to hear. The more diverse the group of people, the better. Then create a letter or email you can send to this group to elicit feedback. Below is a template you may use.

Date:

Dear:

I am currently working on a leadership development program. As part of this program, I am constructing a profile of the ways I add value in various settings. The purpose is to discover and refine the talents, interests, and capabilities unique to me, and explore how I can best put those to work. I have been asked to contact people who know me well and ask them to provide me with up to three stories of when I was at my best. I am inviting you to help me with this exercise. I would greatly appreciate you taking the time to do this for me. This will require you to think about your interactions with me and identify examples and behaviors that show when I was at my best in your eyes.

Please provide specific examples so I can understand the situation and the characteristics you describe. Here is a template of what I am looking for:
One of the ways you add value and make important contributions is _____. For example, I think of the time that you _____.

If you decide to help, I'd be very grateful if you could respond within the next two weeks. If you are not able to help for whatever reason, please let me know that as well so I can contact someone else.

Thank you for your help.

Sincerely,

Once you receive responses, make a chart that tracks the information. Write down one of the themes about you, and then track the examples given to support those. Then try to interpret that information.

For example, you may hear that one of your traits is your creativity. Several people may give examples on that theme (you built a procedure that really helped the organization, and you find new solutions to old problems in the department). List those. Next, work on your interpretation. What do you make of this information. Your interpretation could be that your ideas help build innovation because you bring new vision to old ways.

Keep going recording the insights and looking for commonalities or patterns among them.

Now you're ready to build your Best Self Portrait.

Here is an example of a Best Self Portrait:

> *When I am at my best, I tend to be creative. I am enthusiastic about ideas and I craft bold visions. I am an innovative builder who perseveres in the pursuit of the new. I do not waste energy thinking about missed opportunities or past failures, nor do I take on the negative energy of the insecure or worry about critics. I stay centered and focus on what is possible and important. I use frameworks to help me make sense of complex issues. I can see disparate ideas and integrate them through "yes and" thinking.*

> *So, I make points others do not really see. In doing so, I frame experiences in compelling and engaging ways. I paint visions and provide new ways for people to see. I use metaphors and stories to do this. I*

find the stories in everyday experiences, and people find it easy to understand them. The new images that follow help people act.

In helping others, I try to empathize with them and understand their needs. I give them my attention and energy, but I allow them to be in charge. In exercising influence, I try to enroll people, not force them, in new directions. I invite people to work with me. I use dialogue to help people surface their ideas, and then I weave them together with others until we create knowledge in real time. I ignore symptoms and focus on the deep causes. I help people and groups surface the darkest realities and the most painful conflicts. From these emergent tensions come the energy for transformation. I liberate people from their fears and help them embrace new paths. In all of this, I try to model the message of integrity, growth, and transformation.

Leadership Is Relationship

I really want you to be convinced in the innermost part of your being that effective leadership is built on the solid foundation of sound relationships. If you get that, then the Trust Formula I will soon share with you will become an essential tool for you to build effective relationships not only with the people around you, but with the clients who choose to do business with you and your organization as well.

To start this adventure, let's look at a classic definition of an organization: *a social arrangement that pursues collective goals and controls its own performance.* In a social arrangement, leaders have to answer the question of organization members (WIIFM). For the answer, let's be good business people and look at leadership from the member's perspective.

A couple of well-known leadership experts, James M. Kouzes and Barry Z. Posner, are famous for a survey they produced called "Characteristics of an Admired Leader," in which respondents identified the qualities people want in a leader. This questionnaire, found in their best-selling book *The Leadership Challenge,* has been administered to tens of thousands of people around the globe. The results of this survey have been consistent year in and year out. They seem to indicate that a person must pass several essential tests before others are willing to grant them the title "leader."

The top four characteristics of an admired leader are:

- 88 percent—**Honest**
Truthful, has integrity, trustworthy, has character, is trusting
- 71 percent—**Forward-Looking**
Visionary, foresighted, concerned about the future, sense of direction
- 66 percent—**Competent**
Capable, proficient, effective, gets the job done, professional
- 65 percent—**Inspiring**
Uplifting, enthusiastic, energetic, humorous, cheerful, optimistic, positive about future

Although numerous other characteristics receive votes, and therefore are important to some people, what is most striking is that consistently over time and across continents, only four have continuously received more than 50 percent of the votes. For people to follow someone willingly, most constituents need to believe the leader is Honest, Forward-looking, Competent, and Inspiring.

According to authors Kouzes and Posner:

> When they're performing at their peak, leaders are doing more than just getting results. They're also responding to the expectations of their constituents, underscoring the point that leadership is a relationship and that the relationship is one of service to a purpose and service to people.

A Great Place to Work

Let's overlay more great research by looking at the Great Place to Work model. What makes a great place to work? Based on twenty years of research, trust between managers and employees is the primary defining characteristic of the very best workplaces. It is a place where employees "trust the people they work for, have pride in what they do, and enjoy the people they work with."

I want to remind you of the BAM principle, which corresponds to the research above.

Leaders who make a positive difference in the lives of employees, clients and customers, and the communities they serve generate dynamic results by establishing and cultivating:

- Organizations and teams where employees want to **Belong**.
- Continuous opportunities for **Affirmation**.

• **Meaning** in their organizations that connects to
the hearts and minds of employees and clients.

Now, let's look at the Trust Formula for some really practical implementation.

The Trust Formula

The most important ingredient of relationship-building
doesn't happen by accident. Trust grows as the result of
investing time and energy in some very identifiable and
manageable issues. So how can a motivated leader nurture
trust in the people he or she wants to influence? By focusing
on being emotionally and physically reliable, continuously
improving credibility, creating opportunities to grow more
intimate with the team, and avoiding selfish attitudes and
behaviors.

Prior to giving you the formula, let's go through each of the
factors of trust to understand the importance of each.

- *Reliability* is about whether others see you as
  dependable and behaving consistently. It is about
  the repeated experience and ultimate correlation
  between your promises and your actions.
  Reliability is about clearly communicating
  expectations and fulfilling them. How can you
  improve reliability? By specific commitments to
  some very small and seemingly unimportant
  things, like meetings which have agendas and goals
  that are followed, and champions who are held
  accountable for performance—both good and bad.
- *Credibility* is not just about expertise (a rational
  concept), but also about presence, which refers to

how we look, act, react, and talk about content (an emotional concept). Credibility is rational because it is associated with accuracy, truth, and experience. It is also emotional, relying heavily on honesty and our interpretation of experience. How can credibility be improved? By telling the truth, lovingly. Also, by not exaggerating. At all. Ever. Another tool to improve credibility is to use listening skills to explore and confirm information from team members. We will talk more about listening later, but in general, when you don't know, say so. This can be particularly hard for leaders who often see themselves as being the complete and authoritative problem-solvers.

- *Intimacy* occurs in the realm of emotions and deals with feelings known by and connected to another person. People trust those with whom they are willing to talk about difficult agendas. The most common failure in building trust is the lack of intimacy. Want to improve the level of intimacy in your relationships? Try taking risks first to share your own emotions.

- *Self-orientation* is determined by how much more interest there is in taking care of oneself rather than others. Selfishness is what kills any collateral you have built in the other areas. You can manage self-orientation by using listening skills. Listen to another's story before you tell yours. Take responsibility for your actions. Be honest about what you want and why. Make sure it benefits the organization. Declare that the buck stops with you.

Now let's put all the factors together:

$$Trust =$$
$$(Reliability + Credibility + Intimacy)$$
$$X\ Time$$
$$/\ Self\text{-}Orientation$$

This important equation means that the amount of trust you build as a leader is a function of your reliability, credibility, and intimacy over time divided by how self-oriented you act.

Take Care of Your Team First

Contrary to popular belief, the most important person in your organization is *not* your customer. We already established that you as the leader are the most important organizational asset. But after the leader, it's not the customers. It's your team.

Some leaders might say the customer is the most important person in their organization. That's wrong and destructive. Customers and constituents want what's best for them. They are always answering the question "What's In It for Me?" That's the way it should be. That's their part in the business equation. But the customer making a decision in his or her best interest is neither always right nor the best source of strategy advice.

The organization's role is to satisfy the wants and needs of the customers you want that will benefit both the customer and the organization. Your job as the leader is to ensure that your team understands clearly what every player's role is in the financial model that gives your organization life.

The constituent is important.

The employee is more important.

Your customers look out for themselves. Your team members must consider and balance the best interests of the customer and the organization. For the organization to be vibrant, growing, and profitable, your team members must know the reasons and then have the tools to care for the organization's customers like you want them to.

Your team members can take good care of your clients effectively, but only if you care more about your employees than you do for your customers. What you do and how you act always speaks louder than the Standard Operating Procedures you endorse or your published Rules or any email you distribute with specific directions on how your team members are supposed to behave. Once your team knows you care about them and understands why and how they should care for the people who do business with the organization, then they will take care of customers. And they will care for your customers only as well as you care for them.

The only reason any right-thinking leader hires anybody is to get something important done. But there's a lot more to adding people to your team than just completing assigned tasks. People are expensive. They require nurturing. They crave attention. They want to be consulted. A few may even want your job.

People cause trouble. You will have to fire someone you've invested in, and it will hurt both of you. You must lead them all, getting the whole bunch to move in one direction while they are all asking themselves: What's in It for Me? Getting and keeping the best players is hard work and you must know that it's one of your most important tasks. If you don't like people, consider a different place in your organization. Being the leader requires that you immerse yourself, body and soul, in people.

You must give them a reason to want to be a significant part of your team. People want to be a member of a group that values their contribution. All people need a tribe. They want a sense of Belonging. Remember Belonging? And Affirmation? And Meaning? You must give them opportunities to perform and succeed. When they do succeed, sometimes even when they are even close to succeeding, you must praise the effort and the good parts of the result.

Your success depends on their success and theirs on yours. You are joined at the heart. The more you invest yourself in them, the more they will work for you and the meaning you give them. Be sure to give them Meaning too. As you dive into this incredibly important aspect of the game, get it in your head that you must have people to get the work done. They multiply your energy. They make your ideas better.

Think about the last time you were either angry or frustrated. While driving, the car in front of you cuts in abruptly and too close for your comfort. Your significant other doesn't say the meal you cooked was the best chicken tortilla soup she has ever had. What happened? Or maybe, what didn't happen? Anger and frustration occur because someone didn't act the way you thought he or she should. The driver who cut in front of you should have signaled and then waited politely for you to open a little space so he could move into traffic properly. It didn't happen. Because you don't normally cook, you were expecting your significant other's eyes to light up with delight the moment the spoonful of soup touched her taste buds. It didn't happen. It wasn't what you were expecting. You are frustrated.

**Anger and frustration are
unfulfilled expectations.**

I have trouble thinking about a time when my anger or frustration was not linked to my expectations. I think we all would live a lot longer, with less anger, and with a drop in our frustration levels if we would manage expectations better by sharing them. Doing this would surely increase goodwill and maybe even world peace. As a leader, you need to be intentional about sharing your expectations for behavior, for job performance, for what someone is going to do.

Share what you want and then ask for feedback, "What are you thinking?"

You can then either adjust your expectations or try to manage the other's performance. You give yourself more options. If you determine that the other person may not or cannot fulfill your expectations, you can choose to adjust accordingly. Good leaders don't assume the other person understands what they want. They don't assume their communication is so good or that what they are asking for is so common sense that anyone would understand it.

Tool: The Position Mandate, Communicating Great Expectations

A tremendous amount of energy is spent on finding and implementing the best ways to create environments in which team members can be most productive. Most of the time we hire or promote someone with a general feel-good discussion of why we chose them to do a job. Often a leader tells a new employee what he must do to succeed at the job but almost always leaves out why it must be done. The jobholder is so excited, or maybe intimidated, that he or she doesn't even think to ask why this job is important enough for the organization to pay to get it done.

Next time you play a board game, check out the rules. There is often more detail there on how to play and how to win than what we give the people we are paying to play in our organization! What if we could improve the performance of not just the newbies we hire, but even those who have been with our organization for a while?

Why not regularly share:

- Why you hired them (i.e., why their job is important).
- What your expectations are (i.e., what success looks like).
- What they need to be able to do to help the team win.

The Position Mandate gives the leader and the jobholder the opportunity to define what is critical to job success. It gives everyone involved information that is meaningful, affirming, and applicable to doing meaningful work. Because the foundation for an effective working relationship is a shared commitment to ideas, values, and goals, this tool establishes for the leader and the employee a set of negotiated and agreed-upon behaviors through which important tasks will get done—the bottom line for hiring any and every employee.

As the leader, you are investing time and money into hiring someone you expect to bring more to the party than what he or she costs. How are you going to evaluate your return-on-investment? The person who is choosing to follow you wants to succeed. Nobody takes a job with the intent of failing. The best thing you can do for that person is early and often share what terrific performance looks like.

Like baseball legend Yogi Berra said, "If you don't know where you're going, you will probably end up somewhere else." Instead, end up where you and your employee want to be and avoid anger and frustration along the way.

The Position Mandate is composed of three critical parts:

1. Position
The Positional Why explains why this position exists.

2. Future Facts
The Future Facts for the position describe what optimum performance looks like.

3. Measurement
Measurements establish the metrics for both the leader and the position-holder so they can know if performance equals success.

The Why for the position clarifies the job's core purpose in the format verb/ target/outcome. This is the big picture of what should be accomplished in this position as a contributor to the success of the organization.

The first, basic ingredient of any effective collaboration is sharing the meaning of this Position. This Why provides a framework upon which to hang the details.

Good leaders share in detail what they want to happen and then ask for feedback about how the other person is going to accomplish the task. They don't assume. A little extra work on clarity results in a payoff well worth the investment.

The second ingredient is sharing your expectations in the form of Future Facts for the specific job. Remember, Future Facts are positive statements with present tense verbs that describe in detail really good performance, as if everything were working in your favor, on some fictional day in the future. In this section you are creating optimistic facts that reflect what happens in the future, on the team member's best day, if he or she produces what you want and more. Don't confine your thinking to what is currently happening or what might be accomplished. Instead, paint a word picture of what incredible performance will look like if the team member performs in keeping with your organization's Why.

The third critical ingredient of an effective Position Mandate is Measurement. Everyone wants to make a significant contribution. Measurement defines how that contribution will be evaluated. To determine what a measurement will look like, go to your Future Facts and find things that are tangible and are a result of make the Future Fact a reality.

After you have developed the Position Mandate for a team member, the two of you should clarify metrics of performance that are measurable today, ensuring the measurement criteria for each Future Fact are accurate and agreed-upon indicators of achievement.

An example of specific measurements of Why, Future Facts, and Measurement in a Position Mandate for a president of an organization might be:

Position Why
The president shepherds our company's relation-ships, profitability, and operational structure, creating a collaborative environment that fosters innovation.

Future Fact
All our clients will be 100 percent satisfied with our company's services within one year of this date.

Measurement
Our company's satisfaction rating will be 10 percent higher among my East Coast clients by the end of next quarter using the Net Promoter Score (more on Net Promoter Scores later).

Communication Is Never the Message You Send

I had a pastor-friend who after the Sunday morning church service would stand outside the sanctuary and greet members who were leaving the church. He told me he was touched each week by what people would say about his sermons, thanking him for specific things he said that spoke right to where they lived and pointed them in the right direction.

He said the amazing thing was well over half the time what people thanked him for, he neither said nor even insinuated. People hear what they want to hear. What others hear is determined by their culture, experience, mood, knowledge, and a little bit by what you meant to say. We all have asked someone to run an errand for us only to have that person return without what we wanted or without accomplishing the desired task.

Almost all of us think we are adequate or even good communicators. The fact is that without asking the receiver what he or she heard, it just doesn't matter how good a communicator we think we are, we don't know what was heard without asking the other person to repeat it. And then, to make sure we are communicating we must invest time and words clarifying meanings, terms, and intentions. The investment of a bit of time and energy can save a lot of pain, money, and energy.

When you ask someone to do something, follow up the request with, "I just want to be sure I am doing a good job communicating with you, so tell me what you heard or what you think I want you to do."

Communication is never the message you send; it is the message received.

Your Success Is Directly Proportional to the Number of Difficult Conversations You Are Willing to Have

I don't like confrontation. When people are tense, I am uncomfortable. And I don't like being uncomfortable. I like happy. I like it when the whole team works well together, and we are winning and feeling good about ourselves and each other. The thing is, no day goes by without things happening that create problems. Things get said that are not helpful. Words and actions are misinterpreted. Team members are avoided. People take sides. The workplace becomes a candidate for a reality TV show.

What is the right response to uncomfortable or painful situations? Let it go, and it will work itself out? Maybe. But probably not. Experience tells me that the ignored and unattended problem will grow and morph into a much bigger deal requiring more time and attention (some of your scarce resources) than if you had just taken care of it early on. Identify issues early and move quickly to solve them.

When I wrote that your organization is a direct reflection of you, I made the case that your actions and values set the standard for behavior. If you act wisely to solve difficult problems quickly, you also let the team know what behaviors are helpful to making the organization's *Why* happen. They see that quick and decisive actions on problems that affect the performance of the whole team are important. You set the standard for what is good and acceptable performance.

Your organization's success is directly proportional to the number of difficult and uncomfortable conversations you as the leader are willing to have.

Tool: The GROW Model

Leaders coach team members to achieve their best. As coach, you typically help your team members solve problems, make better decisions, learn new skills, and progress in their roles. While some leaders are fortunate enough to get formal training as coaches, most are not. They must develop coaching skills on their own. Now this may sound daunting. But if you arm yourself with some proven techniques, find opportunities to practice, and learn to trust your instincts, you can become a better coach and thereby enhance your team's performance.

One proven approach that helps with this is the GROW Model. Though the model has been around for a while, I appreciate the work Mindtools.com has done in describing it. They explain how GROW is an acronym for **G**oal, current **R**eality, available **O**ptions, and **W**ill. The model is basically a simple yet powerful framework for structuring a coaching session.

What is the **Goal**?

- When you, as a leader, coach your team members,

you usually will have some expert knowledge to offer. Also, it's your job to guide the selection of options that are best for your organization and veto options that are harmful.

- With your team member, define and agree on the goal or outcome to be achieved. Help your team member define a goal that is specific, measurable, and realistic. In doing this, it is useful to ask questions like: "How will you know you have achieved that goal?" and "How will you know the problem is solved?" The first thing every great problem solver does is clearly define the problem or opportunity, at least to get started. This is a dynamic process. In other words, the more we explore and understand, the more we will know. And the result of this process is that everything, even the definition of the problem, may change. That's a good thing. We want to make good decisions, and good decisions are dependent upon good information.

- Define the problem or opportunity as concisely and clearly as possible in the form of a goal. Think of using the definition of a good story to help you. A good story is about a sympathetic character who, to get something valuable or important, overcomes obstacles. Write a description of what you or your organization want to accomplish and why that is important. Be specific, make it measurable, and tie accomplishment to a date.

Once you have a clear goal in mind, brainstorm what your current **Reality** looks like.

- What are the things keeping you or your

organization from getting what is wanted? Make a list of all the obstacles in your way or things contributing to keeping you from the goal. Ask your team member to describe the current reality. This is a very important step. Too often people try to solve a problem without fully considering the starting point, and they are missing some of the information they need to solve the problem effectively. As the team member tells you about her current reality, the solution may start to emerge.

- Useful coaching questions include: What is happening now? What, who, when, how often? What is the effect or result of that?

Explore the **Options**

- Considering your goal and how reality is keeping you from getting something valuable or important, what options do you have? Start this process by brainstorming possibilities. Write down every possibility that comes to mind, without judgment. Once you have compiled a sizable list, combine your ideas into an option that is the best current alternative for you to focus your energies on achieving. Explore the many possible options you have for solving the problem. Help your team member generate as many good options as possible and discuss these. While you may eventually offer your suggestions, let your team member offer hers first, and let her do most of the talking.
- Typical questions used to establish the Options are: What else could you do? What if this or that constraint were removed? What are the benefits

and downsides of each option? What factors will you use to weigh the options?

Get Agreement to the **Will**

- By examining current reality and exploring the options, your team member will now have a good idea of how she can achieve the goal. That's great, but not enough! Your final step as coach is to get your team member to commit to specific actions. By doing this, you will help the team member establish her will and motivation.
- Useful questions are: So what will you do now? And when? What could stop you from moving forward? And how will you overcome it? Will this address your goal? How likely is this option to succeed? What else will you do?
- Ask them to write a positive statement of what they will do. Make sure the statement is measurable, describes what great performance will look like, and sets a date for projected accomplishment or review.

The two most important skills for a coach are the abilities to ask good questions and to listen well. Avoid asking closed-ended questions like, "Did that cause a problem?" Instead, ask open-ended questions like, "What effect did that have?" Be prepared with a list of questions for each stage of the GROW process.

Listen well and let your team member do most of the talking. Remember that silence is valuable thinking time; you don't always have to fill silence with the next question. A great way to practice using the GROW model is to address your own challenges and issues. When you are stuck with something, use the technique to coach yourself. By practicing with your own challenges and issues, you will learn how to ask good questions of others.

Chapter Takeaways:

1. Leadership requires that you understand that you are not equipped to do everything well and you need others with specific complimentary strengths to make your organization successful. You must know your strengths and those of your decision-making team.

2. You are the lid for your organization. You are the constraint to growth, profitability, and success.

3. Organizations are all about people.

4. Leadership is relationship. Relationship is built on trust.

5. Use the GROW model to address performance issues.

STRATEGY

Chapter Goal: *Supply the tools to create a culture of performance in which your team is always working toward the organization's Why—successfully employing scarce and precious resources to close the gaps between current realities and future goals.*

We were a large employer in a small town. We had access to hardworking, solid people, but I don't think anyone on our team would say we were in, or even near, the cultural center of the universe. We had trouble attracting and keeping talented professional people, especially technically qualified research and development chemists who were critical to our competitiveness and product creation. Few people were interested in coming to a small town in Oklahoma when basically the same opportunities were available in big cities.

Also not in our favor, we were a small manufacturer in a declining business niche. Our product sales were growing partly because competitors were getting out of the business. We were heavily regulated by both OSHA and the EPA.

Our products were hazardous to health and the environment if not handled correctly. It was not a romantic business that attracted the best and brightest. I was the CEO to be sure, but I was only qualified because I had asked for the job and perhaps because I had done most every role in the organization at one time or another.

We were fair-to-good at what we did, but not great. And yet we still had to compete. We wanted not just to survive, but to grow. We wanted to make money and have fun. But how? What strategy could take the limited resources and opportunities available to us, differentiate us from our dwindling set of competitors, develop appealing new products and services, and make us attractive to customers?

I have heard it said that a clear vision + excellent systems = success. While I am not sure the formula always works, it does have some truth to it, as our company discovered almost by accident.

The first thing I did shortly after becoming the boss was to gather all my decision-makers at an offsite location for our very first strategic planning meeting. What a meeting! Nobody in our company had ever thought of gathering all the key players together to talk honestly and openly about:

- What we had (Reality)
- What we wanted (Future Facts)
- How to fill the gap between what we had and
  what we wanted (Strategy)

So we met. It was emotional. And it was painful. But we came up with a short-term strategy or game plan to take our limited resources of knowledge, money, equipment, and situation and apply those things to their best and highest use, hoping for a financial and cultural return.

What we came up with was not radically innovative, groundbreaking, or even wildly progressive to anyone outside our small business niche, but it was the first step of a long and arduous journey to steadily improving every aspect of our organization. We developed goals in each of the four critically important aspects of any business or organization:

- Team—culture, training, hiring, promoting, evaluating
- Finances—profitability, cash management, costs, accountability
- Systems—information, reporting, project management
- Customers—getting new ones and keeping old ones

We repeated that process year after year with varying degrees of success. I am pleased to say that even years later, the small manufacturing business I led is now a major player in its areas of focus. They even expanded the organization in products, services, and locations. They continue to make money and have fun.

Closing the Gap

What's the opposite of strategy? Reaction—the mojo of many organizations. For leaders of these companies, "strategy" depends on reacting to immediate circumstances. What customers are demanding immediate attention? What systems are the most broken? What employee or team is not getting critically important jobs done? Whatever is on fire gets the most attention. And there is always something on fire. Since most leaders are conditioned to respond aggressively to emergencies, they naturally rally resources to get the problem fixed.

But as soon as one crisis gets addressed, another crisis shouts for their attention. Responding to getting problems fixed or getting customers satisfied is very hard work. Really hard work. And there is usually some level of satisfaction with this type of leadership because it means we are "busy getting stuff done." But maybe the wrong stuff? Maybe working way too hard at getting the wrong things accomplished?

Strategy demands that we stop unintentionally reacting to whatever is in front of us and instead thoughtfully examine exactly what we want the organization to accomplish with the limited and precious resources at hand. Strategy requires the intellectual discipline of objectively evaluating what we have in relation to what we really want. It develops a game plan to use our valuable and finite resources to achieve the Why (in one clear, concise, and call-to-action sentence) and Future Facts of the organization. It means working smarter to close the gap between current realities and desired objectives.

Culture Beats Planning

One of the things I looked forward to every year as a leader was getting our decision-makers together to work on a strategic plan for the next year. What fun. We assigned homework. We gathered information from our customers and employees. We wrote stuff on poster paper and put it all over the walls of the conference room where we worked. We wrote hundreds of goals that were worthy and inspiring.

Being together, talking about what we were going to do together, was better than drugs or alcohol. We wrote SMART goals (more on those later) and shared the plan with all our team members at all locations. As far as I could tell, we got a lot of mileage out of planning and the plan. We got a lot done that we planned on. The trouble was that shortly after we put the plan together and shared it with employees, it ended up in a binder on my bookshelf not to be opened until the next year when we started preparing for the next planning session.

But we still achieved good results even though we didn't follow the big business formula of managing by objectives. How did that happen? I am sure many of the right things still got done because we talked often about what the right things were, what was strategically important, who was doing what, and when. In other words, a lot of the right stuff got done because it really was out in front of the team on a regular basis.

But more than that, we had a culture of open discussion, personal and group accountability, and transparency. Our stated, agreed upon Why in one clear, concise and call-to-action sentence, Rules, and Future Facts kept us on track despite our inability to always adopt what might have been best practices for business. Gathering the perceived movers and shakers and sharing with them critical information about our organization had inadvertently initiated a culture where employees' input was incorporated into the decision-making process.

And they wanted more.

Tool: Huddles

Your team will win because they are clear about their role and invested in making the Why in one clear, concise, call-to-action sentence of the organization a reality. It is your job to communicate that goal line over and over in terms your team understands and can get passionate about.

You may have a game plan for success. But stuff happens. Situations change. Customers and people are fickle. It's critical that you and your team get together often to adjust for changes in situations, performance, and availability of resources.

Huddles are simply well structured, concise meetings in which the details of the game at hand are reviewed and resources allocated or reallocated for success. They are simply very short, to-the-point meetings that work. You will have to determine the frequency of your Huddles. I suggest starting with weekly. They are an important tool to reallocate resources as things change.

Here are questions to ask that will give you a foundation for what makes a good Huddle (read any meeting):

- Do you have an agenda for your meeting?
- Did you send out the agenda prior to the meeting?
- Don't ever ask players to come to a meeting that doesn't have an agenda.
- Does your meeting have a clear, measurable goal? What is it?
- If you made assignments, does each attendee know what contributions he or she needs to bring to the meeting?
- Did you only invite team members to the meeting

who have a direct effect on whether the goal is achieved?

- Did you specify a start and end time for the meeting and hold to the schedule?
- Don't penalize those who show up on time by waiting for stragglers before starting a meeting. End the meeting at the time promised. Everyone has other things to do.
- Did you close the meeting with action items and the champion(s) assigned to each item?
- Is a meeting necessary or can the information be shared in a way other than a face-to-face meeting?

Exercise: Strategy in Five Steps

Strategy is intentionally allocating scarce and precious resources for their highest and best use in pursuit of making your Why a reality using Future Facts and SMART goals. When you and your team develop Strategy, you are "pre-thinking" what you want and how you're are going to get it with your organization's scarce and precious resources. Your success as a leader and even that of your organization is determined by how well your scarce and precious resources are allocated for their highest and best use in pursuit of making focused SMART goals happen.

Here are five steps for putting together an effective Strategy.

1. Start with your **Why**
2. Then review your **Rules**
3. Build **Future Facts**
4. Create **SMART goals**
5. **Measure**, **Measure**, **Measure**

Then adjust and repeat.

The good news is to create your Strategy, you have already developed your Why, Rules, and Future Facts for the organization. But let's review the essentials of Future Facts because we will use them again as the foundation of the SMART goals that will make up your Strategy.

Remember that Future Facts are positive statements with present tense verbs that describe, in some detail, what really good performance will look like in the future if everything were working in your favor. Future Facts are like pre-seeing a particular future, and it is an essential tool for any ambitious leader. It's an essential tool when leaders need to communicate in a way that lifts the fog for others on the team, enabling everyone to respond more quickly and safely in a changing environment. Future Facts help give meaning and purpose to the effort of getting important things done, and it's possible to have a lot more fun when the team can clearly see what success looks like.

As you and your team think about Strategy, there are four critical areas for Future Facts where you will want to focus your energy. I have borrowed the following concept from Kaplan and Norton's, "Balanced ScoreCard" in the *Harvard Business Review*.

The following examples come from the most recent company I was able developed, DecisionGrid. We provided financial services for clients to help them succeed and thrive.

Financial
What's the priority? Is it more dollars coming in or profit improvement for the transactions that occur naturally?

Future Fact Example: *While our financial perfor-*
mance is always positive, it is not our goal to be
wildly profitable. Our financial goal is to develop a
financial model that equally benefits all our stake-
holders—clients, employees, and owners.

Systems Excellence
What must the organization do repeatedly and with
quality?
Future Fact Example: *Our systems for compiling*
and sharing timely and accurate information are
constantly evolving in response to our stewardship
partners' needs and those of the people they serve.
We are constantly evaluating our processes and
systems to improve them. We want our clients to
improve their processes and systems too. As a result,
our systems and complementary services set the
industry benchmark.

Team Members
What do we need for and from our team culture,
our approach to our work, and our customers?
Future Fact Example: *We constantly affirm that our*
team members are the primary reason for organiza-
tional success and growth. They are "engaged" in
supplying the accurate and timely information our
stewardship partner clients require for success. We
choose and then cultivate employees to "own" the
services our organizations supplies to its partner
clients. Our culture is one of ownership, participa-
tion, growth, and cooperation.

Customers
How do we treat them? How do we want them to

perceive us? Which ones do we want? Which ones do we want to keep?

Future Fact Example: *Our customers experience lively and ongoing growth based on the inspired decisions they can make from the timely and accurate information we supply. We choose to offer our services only to stewardship partner clients that make a net contribution to improving the quality of life for their clients and their team members.*

Once you have built your Future Facts, spend some significant time comparing what you want to what you have. Consider using some form of a SWOT Matrix (information about that tool follows in this chapter). You will discover gaps between what your Future Facts describe and reality. There will likely be some significant gaps you will want to close quickly. Choose only three or four that will give you the biggest Return On your Investment (ROI) in the shortest amount of time and build SMART goals to help you implement your Strategy.

Tool: SMART Goals

Most leaders will agree that establishing goals is important to the success of any endeavor. Studies show that setting goals significantly improves the likelihood of important things getting done. While writing good effective goals is not complicated, following the tried and true format of SMART goals will add terrific value to the goals you do set and improving both execution and results.

SMART goals are:

Specific

Goals should be straightforward and emphasize what you want to happen. Specifics help focus efforts and clearly define what you are going to do. They provide the Who, What, Why, and How of the SMART goal.

• WHO is going to be the go-to person with bottom line responsibility for getting the goal accomplished?

• WHAT are you going to do? Use action words such as direct, organize, coordinate, lead, develop, plan, build, etc.

• WHY is this important to do now? What do you want to ultimately accomplish?

• HOW are you going to do it? (By . . .)

• Make sure the goals you set are specific and clear. For example, a SMART goal for your health might be setting a specific goal to walk five miles at an aerobically challenging pace, four days per week, for the next two months.

Measurable

If you can't measure it, you can't manage it. In the broadest sense, the whole goal statement is a measure for the project. If the goal is accomplished, there is success. However, there are usually several short-term or small measurements that can be built into the goal. In our game analogy, think of these as first downs. Small wins motivate people toward bigger goals. Choose a goal with measurable progress so you can see the change occur. Be specific: "I will read three books of at least 300 pages before my birthday" shows the specific target to measure. "I want to read more" is not nearly as measurable. Establish concrete criteria for measuring progress toward the attainment of each goal you set. When you measure your progress, you stay on track, reach your target dates, and experience the exhilaration of achievement that spurs you toward the effort required to reach your goals.

Action-Oriented

When you identify goals that are important to you, you begin to figure out ways to make them come true. You develop the attitudes, abilities, skills, and financial capacity to reach them. You begin to see previously overlooked opportunities to bring yourself closer to the achievement of your goals. An Action-Oriented goal produces results. Identify what you or your team will DO to produce results. Don't just think or talk about making an area of your organization better. Decide what you will *do* to make it better. Action-Oriented goals can be measured. Use action verbs in the goals you set.

Relevant

SMART goals must be relevant to your organization's Why, Rules, and Future Facts. Your SMART goals must always answer the WIIFM question for everyone concerned. If the goal is not relevant or doesn't help to make your Why a reality, you should not allocate scarce and precious resources to getting it done.

Tied-to-a-Date

Set a time frame for the goal: next week, in three months, by the next awards ceremony. If you don't set a time, the commitment is too vague. It tends not to happen because you feel you can start at any time. Without a time limit, there's no urgency to start acting now. Putting an end point on your goal gives you a clear target to work toward.

By creating Future Facts (in the critical areas of Financial, Customers, Team, and Systems) and SMART goals you can develop an effective Strategy to help make your Why happen.

You and your team have pre-thought what you want to achieve and how you will get there with your organization's scarce and precious resources. You have significantly improved your chances of success!

BHAGs Inspire and Small Improvements Win

BHAG is an acronym for a **B**ig **H**airy **A**udacious **G**oal. The idea is that teams often respond to a seemingly unreachable goal that stretches all available resources up to and sometimes past the perceived breaking point. It's sort of like telling a group of people they can't do something in order to motivate them to extraordinary performance. If done well, a BHAG can be exactly what an organization needs to unite the players to pursue extraordinary behavior.

In the 1960s President Kennedy's goal to put a man on the moon by the end of the decade was a BHAG. Even though the Soviets had recently put a man in space, few people thought that leaving a footprint on the surface of the moon was possible in such a short amount of time. Many things had to be accomplished (continuous, incremental improvement) before such a thing was possible. Nonetheless, the President had captured the imagination of the nation and as history records, the United States planted its flag on the surface of the moon on July 20, 1969.

Without a doubt, BHAGs presented well and at the right moment can inspire and facilitate extraordinary performance. But while there's a place for the inspirational leadership tool called a Big Hairy Audacious Goal, let me encourage you to also be a good steward of your limited resources by insisting that on a regular basis your team focus on the less romantic concept of gradual and consistent improvement. In my experience, few leaders have either the vision or the requisite presentation skills to create an inspiring BHAG.

But all leaders can create and drive ongoing incremental improvement. Small improvements lead to wins too! An effective way to focus on consistent gradual improvement is for you and your team to regularly evaluate the good and bad of all your resources and consider what the organization faces in terms of competition, market opportunities, and regulations. One way to do this is to identify your organization's Strengths, Weaknesses, Opportunities, and Threats and distill them into a SWOT Analysis.

Exercise: SWOT Analysis

A **SWOT** Analysis is a planning tool used to evaluate the **S**trengths, **W**eaknesses, **O**pportunities, and **T**hreats of an organization. Much of what follows is based on the explanations of Jan King in *Business Plans to Game Plans* and Stephen Fairley and William Zipp in *The Business Coaching Toolkit*. A SWOT Analysis involves focusing on the Why *in one clear, concise, call-to-action sentence* of your organization and then identifying the internal and external factors that are favorable and unfavorable to achieving the Why. The Strengths and Weaknesses portion of the SWOT looks at factors inside your organization, while the Opportunities and Threats portion focuses on issues outside of it. To complete your SWOT Analysis, answer the questions below:

The Strengths/Weaknesses portion of the SWOT Analysis helps you get a clear picture of factors within your organization that affect its health.

Strengths

Strengths are your core competencies, those things you do better than any of your competitors or that really tie together all the products or services you offer in a unique way. What internal structures or expertise do you have that are a special source of pride? This becomes the center for determining what you will do in the future. You want to constantly build on the things you already do particularly well. What do clients and outside partners (i.e., suppliers, business partners) say is your top strength? What do you think the organization does better than anyone else? To what do you attribute your organization's current level of success? How do you measure success? What are the top five reasons a client should buy from you and not from your competitors?

Weaknesses

For everything you see clearly or do well, there is something you can't see so clearly or do so well. Some of these weaknesses you can change, but others you can't. Where do you need to build your company? What is holding you back or creating a bottleneck for everyone else? If you choose to spend money or other resources in one direction, in what other directions might you be tolerating or creating weaknesses?

Work on making your weaknesses irrelevant, not on changing them to strengths. What are two or three areas your team members complain about the most? What are two or three areas your customers complain about the most? What does your competition do better than you? If you could change three things about your company, what would you change? What would you change first? Why?

Ask yourself whether the following items are strengths or weaknesses for your company:

- Product quality
- Quality of the management staff
- Quality of technical staff
- Brand name
- Planning process
- Quality of staff performance management system
- Profitability
- Availability of cash for growth
- Quality of marketing and sales efforts
- Compliance with legal requirements
- Facilities
- Operations Staff morale

Next, let's look at the Opportunities/Threats portion of the SWOT. Analysis looks at factors outside your organization that can have a profound effect on its ultimate success. Scanning the external environment clarifies your future opportunities and forces your organization to face problems that could threaten its survival if not considered.

Opportunities
The most difficult thing about opportunity is recognizing it. The adage about opportunity only knocks once does apply

in many cases, so you need to see it—and be able to act on it—when it comes.

What are your greatest challenges in the changing environment of the business niches you serve? How will new technologies help you? What will your customers need in the future that you can supply? What opportunities will open globally? Are there people who are not competitors who already have a relationship with your potential customers that might be attractive partners? What needs to be done to position your company as being on the cutting edge as a leader in the industry?

How could you take advantage of:

• Changes in technology
• Changes in the marketplace, both locally and nationally
• Changes in government policy related to your field
• Changes in social patterns, population movement, changing demographics, lifestyle
• Changes in buying cycles and needs like faster turnaround time, lower prices, more selection, better quality, customization requests, etc.

Threats
As with weaknesses, there are some threats you can minimize and others you can't. You need to do all you can to control the threats you can predict and prepare for the ones you can't.

What outside your control could threaten your existence? How might new technology hurt you? What in the political environment might threaten you? Will ups or downs in the economy hurt you? What in your physical environment might threaten you? What are the five greatest obstacles your organization currently faces? How does rapidly changing technology affect your business model? What are the current trends in your industry? What are you currently doing to identify, train, and retain your top team members? What would happen if your top three people were hired away by your most aggressive competitor? How long would it take you to be up and running if your company were robbed, vandalized, or burned down? What is the worst-case scenario you fear the most?

Consider the following factors:

- Market limitations
- Lack of availability of capital
- Problems with suppliers
- Natural disasters
- Location challenges
- Quality of labor pool
- Revolutionary changes in the industry
- Government regulations
- Technological changes

Tool: Build an Inspired Playbook

Early in my budding career, I was driving a pickup truck with three 55-gallon drums of flammable chemicals from our manufacturing plant in Oklahoma to a very anxious customer in Kansas. It was a foggy, dark early morning on a two-lane highway, and I couldn't see three yards in front of me.

When you are driving your organization in the fog, and you don't know where you are going, and you might explode any second, you drive both slowly and cautiously. An inspired Playbook gives you and your team a clear and simple description of where your organization wants to go and how it's going to get there so you and your organization can accomplish cool stuff and make money doing it.

You may be asking, "What is a Playbook, and why does my organization need one?" I'll answer that question by asking you a question: "How do you feel when you drive on your favorite highway on a crystal-clear day when you can see for miles?" You are able to be much less stressed, more confident, and able to cover more road.

Likewise, a Playbook is a critical tool in turning a foggy and fearful outlook into a clear and full-speed-ahead view for all your stakeholders: employees, customers, and constituents.

A Playbook is a document that simply and clearly describes where the organization wants to go and how it is going to get there. A Playbook is helpful when we consider the truth of the the following axiom:

> *The success of any endeavor is determined by how well scarce and precious resources are applied for their highest and best use in pursuit of a goal.*

Let's look at the ingredients of that statement:

First, do you know what success looks like? Have you written that down? Do your team members know what success looks like?

What are your scarce and precious resources? You'd be on target if you identified knowledge, energy, money, and enthusiasm, among others.

How do you allocate, employ, and use those scarce and

precious resources? Remember the Balanced ScoreCard work by Kaplan and Norton covered earlier in this chapter. Your Playbook clarifies for your team members and other stakeholders how your organization focuses resources on the four areas of your organization that require attention for long-term success.

- Systems
- Culture
- Rules
- Customers

Most organizations and leaders spend much of their time and energy (which are scarce and precious resources) on getting things done without knowing the difference between what's urgent and what's important. A solid Playbook defines what's important and significantly improve focus and efficiency. To build a Playbook, think about how each of the five critical elements of a game apply to your organization.

Remember *The Best Game* model and include the following as chapters:

Goal
This is your Why in once concise, clear, call-to-action sentence.

Rules
These are few, concise, strategic rules for performance behavior that sets the organization apart from competitors.

Players

These communicate performance expectations.

Strategy
Strategies are simple, focused plan for how to apply scarce and precious resources to achieve specific goals.

Measurements
We have to have some way to record and measure our progress and achievement of goals (or lack thereof).

In the first section, you will state your organization's **Goal**/Why. If you like, you can also expand on what it means to you, the team, and stakeholders. What is the goal, what does good performance look like? To what end are we applying scarce and precious resources? How do you know you are having success? The first and most important aspect is to choose a target or goal and focus your scarce and precious resources to get what you want.

The second section communicates one to four strategic **Rules**. Your Rules concisely describe how your team members are to treat each other and your customers.

In the third section, describe what you want from your **Players**. Communicate expectations (anger and frustration are unfulfilled expectations). Describe what your organization expects from team members and what they can expect from the organization.

This section can be a valuable tool in the hiring and employee process. You could outline details such as:

• Our Hiring Process

- How We Compensate Our Team Members (and why that is important)
- A Day in the Life (How We Work)
- Three Keys to Organizational Success (BAM)
- Our Environment
- Our Workday and Our Work Environment

In the fourth **Strategy** section, you describe how you intend to apply scarce and precious resources for their highest and best use in pursuit of your goal. In this section, you describe your product, services, and processes. You might also cover what you believe are your most important policies and procedures, perhaps possibly:

- A List of Services
- Your Pricing Philosophy

The fifth section, which will be important to both employees and your clients, talks about **Measures** such as:

- Your Monthly Metrics and how they relate to what success looks like
- Annual/Net Promoter Score

If you view your Playbook as an ongoing project, reviewing it often with your team members and your clients, it will become an asset to communicating what you want and keeping your team focused on the goal(s) you want to achieve.

Chapter Takeaways:

1. Goals, Strategies, and Action Plans are important tools for any leader. Planning is not an event, it is ongoing.

2. Building a performance culture focused on winning depends upon both you and your team being constantly reminded of the Why, Rules, and Future Facts.

3. Develop a Playbook that will communicate expectations of the essentials of where the organization wants to go, and how you plan to get there.

MEASURES

Chapter Goal: *Measurement is feedback on performance. This chapter will give you tools to determine and use meaningful measurements to assess performance toward goals. You must know how to communicate key measurements to engage players so everyone is focused on the goal during play.*

I told you earlier that what originally qualified me to be a CEO was that I had a Bachelors Degree in English and Education—I could write a good letter— and along the way, I acquired a Master's Degree in Human Relations. Those dubious credentials for the leadership job were supplemented with desire, willingness, a smattering of confidence, and naiveté.

One of the crazy things I started doing soon after I became the boss was to share all the financial information with my team of decision-makers, my executive staff. Because I knew all of them well, I also knew they were smarter and more experienced than I was in their areas. I thought, and was proved right over time, that they would make either the same or better decisions than I would if they were armed with the same information. And they did.

I was amazed at how if I focused on leading well— promoting the principles of how our culture was to operate, focusing attention on our mantra of making money and having fun, and giving employees accurate and timely financial statements—a bunch of well-intentioned, ambitious, fun-loving people could build a successful and profitable enterprise.

We quickly learned that the formula for competing successfully was pretty simple:

Sales Dollars − Expenses = Profits.

It's not rocket science. In fact, it is the same formula every business and organization must follow to successfully compete. Everyone who worked for us learned that same formula. We measured each aspect of the formula and started sharing the fruits of our hard work with all our stakeholder-employees.

And guess what? We got more and more of what we measured and shared! The issue most leaders regularly face is getting employees connected and invested in what they are paid to do.

Gallup polls report the ratio of engaged to actively disengaged employees is twice as many as productively engaged ones. You read that right. For every productive, engaged team member in your company there are two that are "actively disengaged." In other words, you have team members who regularly eat away at any progress toward getting the right stuff done in the right way by the right employees at the right time.

Actively disengaged employees don't make a meaningful contribution to the universal competition formula: Sales Dollars – Expenses = Profits. In fact, their contribution is negative! You would do better without them.

Within the US workforce, Gallup estimates this cost to the bottom line to be more than $300 billion in lost productivity alone. While that number may impress you, think about the following: world-class organizations have an engagement ratio of more than 9 to 1. Nine solid, contributing, passionate players who are invested in getting the right stuff done in the right way by the right people at the right time, versus one slug.

You can get there. There is no silver bullet, but there are a few things you can do to move toward a win.

Competition

When we begin considering the critical ingredients of a game and how they can be applied to leading an organization, many may include the concept of competition. While I am not necessarily discounting competition as a critical ingredient, if you think through what competition is, what purpose it serves, and how to use the concept positively, competition is basically measurement that becomes a benchmark to use toward improvement.

Without a doubt, competition can be used positively to improve the quality of life, but without careful thought it also can damage people and relationships. A leader's job is to build trust-based relationships to get done what is important using the passions, experiences, and knowledge of a group of people.

A leader's job can be painful, and often the decisions that

have to be made are uncomfortable. However, a leader's job is never to do harm, at least in the big picture. Instead, a leader's job is to make the lives of employees and customers always just a little bit better. Using objective measurements, rather than trying to mold competition with all of its variables, is a better way to accomplish this.

Relentless Execution

Most of us don't have a problem with knowing what to do; we have a problem with doing it. We have a problem with execution. We may look busy much of the time. But busyness doesn't matter if the activity is not moving us toward our objective. We need relentless execution toward getting the right stuff done by the right people, in the right way, at the right time, for the right cost. All the strategy in the world won't help you win if you don't execute the plays in the game when needed.

The same is true in organizations. Take all those strategic goals you developed and use them to achieve your organization's goal. Let measurement and competition help you implement your plans!

Did you ever play Slap Jack with a kid? It may be the simplest of card games. The premise, as you may remember, is simply to turn over cards from a shuffled deck, and then as soon as the Jack of clubs shows his face, the first one to slap it gets all the cards underneath. At the end of the game, the person with the most cards wins. Of course, if you slap any other card but a Jack, your opponent gets all the cards beneath the card you mistakenly slapped. It's a simple game, but it's fun.

Why? Because there are clear rules with measurement and

competition. What if all you had to do was slap the Jack? No measurement, no competition, no rush to slap that Jack first, no drive to the get the most cards. Would that be fun? Not very.

Measurement supports relentless execution. It gets other involved. Playing the game and measuring results answers WIIFM for the players.

What Gets Measured Gets Done

Without measurement, improvement or failure is just a feeling. Without measurement, we don't know whether we are losing or gaining weight, winning or losing a game, or solving or exacerbating a problem.

We all want to be successful. We all like to win. We want to stack the odds in favor of getting what we want. So let's be thoughtful and intentional about approaching this critical tool of measurement. What we measure is what we get. Therefore, it's critical to measure the right things to get the right things done.

Some organizations measure when people show up and when they leave. Is showing up and leaving on time all we want? The obvious answer is, of course not. What we want is growth, productivity, creativity, passion, constant improvement, raving customers, profitability, and the like. But how many organizations do you know that measure the right things, much less share the information with the people doing the work? If organizations measure when employees clock in and clock out, what's the message to employees? That the organization wants your bodies on site, but what you do while you're at work is only of secondary importance? It's not the message I want to send if I have a choice.

As the leader, you do have a choice. Measure those things that directly reflect what you are investing energy, time, and money to get. If you are looking for an outcome that is in your favor (and isn't that why you set goals in the first place?), tip the odds that way by building accountability through measuring those things you want to make sure get done.

Think about any sports-related activity. What's important to winning the game gets measured whether it's quantity, as in the number of times a player crosses home plate in baseball, or quality, as in getting the ball in the golf hole by using the fewest number of strokes. Whatever is important gets measured. The focus on reaching the measurable goal.

The same is true in leading an organization. Measure whatever you want more of. And when you measure, measure and communicate publicly with those doing the work. The more important the measurement, the more that measurement should be given the spotlight and center stage, even to the point of basing bonuses and compensation on it. The point is to be thoughtful and proactive about what you measure and how those results are used and shared. Measure all the important stuff in the four critical areas of Balanced Scorecard (covered in Chapter 4) that makes your Why happen. Measure and celebrate all things that are related to your Rules and Future Facts.

No Measurement, No Competition

In games and in business, where there is measurement and competition there is attention to performance. A desire to do your best to win. To use measurement and competition to their best advantage in your organization, measure the right amount of information, measure information directly connected to what you want to accomplish, share measurement results, and encourage positive competition.

Measurement is a critical leadership tool too often unused or misused. However, when measurement is employed well it makes an incredible difference to the outcome. Think of measurement as a leadership tool that gives feedback on performance, which everyone needs. Measurement is essential to a passionate, high-performance work environment.

Let's remember that success is determined by how well scarce and precious resources are invested for their highest and best use in pursuit of a goal. Leaders know we never have all the resources needed to get done the things we want to accomplish. Scarce and precious are time, money, passion, equipment, raw materials, and intelligence. What determines success is how well we take what's available to us and apply it to get what we want. That is the challenge.

Think about your organization for a minute. Let me ask you two tough questions that are essential to your organization's success:

- How do you decide how to allocate your scarce and precious resources for their highest and best return?
- How do you know (measurably) that your organization is having success?

The answer to the first question comes primarily from how well you and your organization define the Why of your enterprise and then the goals you want to achieve that make your mission a reality.

The answer to the second question is measuring the ROI (Return On Investment) of whatever you define as your most important (and expensive) scarce and precious resources as you invest them to accomplish a SMART goal.

What Should We Measure?

Like we learned in the previous chapter, there are four areas that are the foundation for long-term organizational health.

First, measure an important financial number. It's reality that every organization, whether for-profit or not-for-profit, must make at least a dollar. Know your financial engine and decide what it will take to keep it healthy.

Second, measure the quality of the systems important to your organization to ensure the important things gets done well, repeatedly.

Third, measure the quality and contribution of the people you have on your team, whose capabilities and capacities most affect what your organization wants to accomplish.

Fourth, measure how your customers or clients see and experience your organization related to what you want to accomplish.

While measurement and feedback on performance is a critical tool, it also can be misused which is demotivating. Here are some common pitfalls to avoid.

Measuring too much

How many of you can look at a Profit & Loss Statement, a Balance Sheet, and a Cash Flow Statement and then give me an overview of the business that supplied the numbers? Not many, to be sure. It's a fault of financial management thinking that makes those reports way too complicated to be useful to an interested but untrained person. There is usually so much information on those documents no normal person would be interested in picking one up. Instead, focus on measuring—and sharing—the measurements that matter most.

Measuring too little

I have the honor of working with some very successful CEOs. Would you be surprised to know most of them measure almost nothing except knowing how much money is in their bank account and what their total sales dollars are for the month? Most don't know how to utilize financial statements or scoreboards as essential decision-making tools. Instead, focus on measuring—and sharing—the measurements that matter most.

Measuring stuff that has little to do with what we want to accomplish

What's the most important thing your company wants to accomplish? How do you measure getting that most important thing accomplished? Do you measure how well you get done what's most important to get done? What happens if you don't measure what's important? Focus on measuring— and sharing—the measurements that matter most.

If you are starting to feel uncomfortable answering those last few questions, you are in good company. Most organizations don't measure the right stuff. See if the following helps make sense of why measuring the right things are important.

What gets measured at a football game in order of priority? What will you see for sure if you look up at the scoreboard to see how to assess the game? Number of points each team has scored. Time expired, remaining, what quarter is it, and how many time-outs are left. Which team has the ball. What down it is. How many yards are needed for a first down.

There are many more statistics measured not normally on a scoreboard. Why not? Because they are not critically important to winning the game! Measure the right thing, and the right thing gets done. Measure the wrong thing, and the wrong thing gets done. Measure too much, and nothing gets done.

The lesson here: be *very* careful what you measure!

Not sharing measurements to encourage positive competition

Do you know the reason most people hate their jobs? It's not because the job is meaningless. Almost every job has a good reason behind it. It's because leadership fails team members by not explaining why their job is important, what good performance looks like, or what's in it for the person doing the work. Sharing measurement and encouraging positive competition has worked for games since humans started playing together. Why don't we use the principle of measurement and competition in organizations?

Sharing measurements and information that is not actionable

Don't give your team information they don't ask for and can't do anything with. If the information you share motivates you and your team to work on some issue, celebrate some improvement, or stop doing something unprofitable, great! If the information you want to share doesn't initiate some sort of action, save it. If it's not actionable, don't share it.

We Are What We Measure

One of my CEO clients rarely gets involved in the day-to-day operations of his company until someone makes a mistake. Then no matter what group owns the mistake, he dictates a solution that becomes company policy. The result is not only a lot of policies and procedures that few can remember, but the organization is primarily focused on mistakes, or not making mistakes. You can guess what it's like to work there—keep your head down, do what you're supposed to do and nothing more. Turnover is high, and there is little initiative. The organization reflects what the boss measures.

I have another client of a startup whose Why is "Innovation that makes money and changes the world" and whose Future Facts say his organization will win awards for innovation. The business started with nothing, but now they need a trophy case to hold all the awards that have been given by various local and regional sponsors. The clear majority of their small number of employees are focused on coming up with new ideas that will make money. It's a fun place to work. They are making money, and they share in the fruits of what they produce.

The character of the organization is always reflected in what is measured. All of us measure things that we perceive are important. As the leader of your organization, think carefully about what is important to fulfilling your Why, Rules, and Future Facts, and then be intentional about what is measured, communicated, and celebrated. Choosing the right things to measure is critical to success, but doing it well is neither easy nor obvious.

Many of your processes are easy to measure, but if they encourage unhelpful internal departmental competition, they may be counterproductive.

As a young president, one of the first things I took on to solve was our chronic shipping problem. Orders went out late, incomplete, and with mistakes. Without getting the shipping team together (my bad), my Operation VP and I developed an incentive system that measured mistakes, labor efficiency, and turnaround time from order entry to pick up.

It should have worked. And it did, in a way. We enjoyed some improvement in our shipping department simply because we were measuring something, and as pointed out earlier, what gets measured, gets done.

The problem was our manufacturing team needed manpower help from the shipping team in order to get products made, but because the incentive system did not encourage cooperation between teams, nobody in shipping wanted to help. Ouch. We eventually changed the incentive system.

Some metrics are more difficult to measure, but as the leader you must focus your whole team on decisions and actions critical to accomplishing the Why, Rules, and Future Facts. A good measurement is:

- Clear
- Eventually tied to profit
- Applicable to team performance (vs. individual)
- Designed to encourage good decision-making in the best interest of the organization.

Also remember that players function better in environments of Belonging, Meaning, and Affirmation (BAM). Awards are great affirmation and should come as soon after the desired performance as possible. Real-time is best but usually impractical so work hard and spend resources to recognize performance in a timely manner. My experience is that quarterly is the longest effective time period for recognizing success.

Success Promotes Success

At the very first moment my father's business could afford it, he bought a Cadillac. He drove one until the day he died. Being a wannabe hippie, I was never a Cadillac lover, so I asked him in a rather condescending way why he choose to drive a big, long, gas-guzzling land yacht. No doubt, I should have used different words, but instead of ripping my head off, he simply replied, "Successful people like to deal with successful people."

And that ended the conversation. Although at the time I scoffed at the answer, it has obviously stuck with me. And it has stuck with me because it's true, success promotes success. You may recall a commonly repeated phrase in business circles, "Nothing succeeds like success." In his book *Good to Great*, Jim Collins calls it momentum.

However you say it, the principle is true. So how can we use the rule to our advantage? Work at creating situations where wins are relatively easy and quick, and the results of the win contribute to something bigger that favors the organization. Your job is to monitor progress, encourage success, and when it happens, to celebrate so everybody on the whole team hears about it.

Mini-Games

What I described above can often give rise to a Mini-Game, especially when solving a problem has a small window of time from start to finish. Because few people enjoy change, your teams will much more readily embrace new ideas and different behaviors if you can clearly answer WIIFM for them. Setting up Mini-Games with easy, quick, but real wins designed to promote both a win and a solution to a problem is an effective way to initiate a paradigm shift for your team.

Mini-Games have a short, usually no more than four-month horizon, and are designed for groups that have a short-term goal that, when achieved, will benefit either a SMART goal that requires immediate attention. Supervisors and managers can build games around improving team output, efficiency, or number of sales contracts. Rewards can be financial, but also think about rewards that instead have to do with Belonging, Affirmation, and Meaning.

Reaching a goal may get the team something as simple as a t-shirt or a catered lunch or dinner. The reward does not have to be significant in terms of cost. It simply is recognition by the leader of the goal that was accomplished.

Tool: ScoreBoards

I can't think of any game that is any fun if you don't keep score. The score is an indication of performance against a competitor, against a benchmark, or even against your own best effort. In an organization, ScoreBoards can and should be everywhere. Thoughtfully constructed ScoreBoards focus your precious resources on what's important and contribute to the enjoyment of the game and success of the enterprise. However, poorly conceived ScoreBoards can be demotivating. To do ScoreBoards right, keep a couple of principles in mind:

- What gets measured gets done.
- We are what we measure.

Therefore, make sure you are measuring what you want to see happen. Look back at your Future Facts and your Rules. Are the things you are measuring directly helping accomplish what you want to happen? If not, stop. If you measure the wrong things, the wrong things get done. Measure the right stuff, celebrate progress and wins, and you'll discover what a great leadership and management tool ScoreBoards are to get you what you want.

Success doesn't come from a good idea. Success comes from the relentless execution (and constant improvement) of repeatable and efficient processes built on a good idea. Simple ScoreBoards built to measure the effectiveness of the processes are one of your major tools for building Belonging, Affirmation, and Meaning.

ScoreBoards build Belonging, uniting a group of people to work toward achieving a goal.

ScoreBoards offer Affirmation, recognizing your people when they win.

ScoreBoards create Meaning, allowing team members to contribute their gifts, abilities, talents, and knowledge to making something worthwhile happen.

Coach and Train for Financial Literacy

Financial literacy is about understanding money and finances, and being able to confidently apply that knowledge to make effective financial decisions. Knowing how to make sound money decisions is a core life skill. Making good financial decisions affects quality of life, opportunities we can pursue, our sense of security, and the overall economic health of our society.

All your team members can and want to understand how your organization works. Learning the financial language of financial statements is the simplest and best way to make your Players long-term, passionate members of your team. Spending some of your precious and limited resources educating and training your team on how to read and interpret financial statements is an investment in your current and future success. You can pay somebody else who specializes in training for financial literacy, or you can do it yourself.

Whatever you do, get involved with the process so your team members know it is important. Financial statements are not rocket science. It does not take an accountant to create them or read them. As we have talked about before, the formula is simple:

Sales Dollars – Expenses = Profit

That's it. Your job as the leader is to make the complex simple, not the other way around. If you cannot read and explain a financial statement to the team members who have chosen to follow you, you are failing both them and, more importantly, yourself. If all organizations survive and prosper because they take in more dollars than they spend (there's that simple formula again), then *everybody* in the organization must understand how that works in terms of individual team members, subgroups, departments, and the whole organization.

Tool: Financial Statements

How do you know if your venture is successful? Many leaders of growing enterprises will answer that question by saying they have customers and clients, money in the bank account, or new clients every day.

But when I say, "Great. Let's walk through your financial statements for this year and last," I usually get a look like I just asked for a month's supply of some illegal substance. They quickly say they're not up-to-date or they can get them from their accountant up through a couple of months ago.

Ouch. Remember: what gets measured gets done. So based on the responses above, you could measure sales or cash in the bank. My educated guess is that if you are measuring sales, then sales are what's happening. And that's good. It's also probably good that you have cash in the bank.

But what's happening between those two numbers (sales and cash) can either make or break your organization. And most organizations don't have a clue as to what their actual costs are, which means what is happening between when you get money from sales and when you put it in the bank. As the leader, you must be able to answer questions like:

- What does each transaction cost the organization?
- What is the percent return on the dollars you (or someone else) have invested in making the transactions happen?
- How do you know that each person in your organization, including yourself, is worth what you are paying?
- Can you get a better return on your money by putting it in the bank and not working at all?
- But most critically, how do you measure success?

That's where financial statements become vital. And I mean vital in the most literal sense: extremely important, needed by your corporate body to keep living. Almost none of us think of financial statements in those terms. Most leaders think of them as a necessary evil. At best, they are documents you must give to your accountant at the end of the year so your taxes can be filed. At worst, they are documents that might as well have been written in a foreign language, because they are so complicated. And besides, you say, you are a people-person and not good with numbers anyway.

But isn't money one of the most critical and precious resources you have? How do you track where it goes and what it does for you and your organization? Tracking sales dollars and the cash balance in your checking account may keep the doors open, but that is not the success formula of any dynamic organization.

The answer to how to be a good steward is to understand that financial statements are pretty straightforward and easy to understand once you know the formulas. Your financial statements tell the financial health of the organization factually and without emotion. They can indirectly reveal the more intangible but critically important aspects of the company, like whether your people are getting the right things done, at the right time, in the right way, by the right people, and at the right cost to make your Why (in a clear, concise, call-to-action statement) happen. Wow! What a tool.

Becoming proficient at reading and using financial statements is critically important to your success in leading your organization to sustainability, profit, and effectiveness. However, the topic cannot be contained in a few paragraphs. If you need to grow in this area, I would encourage you to look at some outside training or perhaps getting a mentor in this area. A good mentor can help translate the often obscure and confusing aspects of financial statements into the simple formulas and information they are meant to convey.

Suffice it to say that you can and should invest energy and time into pursuing financial literacy for you and your team. The investment will give you unexpected and rich returns!

Tool: Net Promoter Score

How do you measure the impact your business has on people? How do you know whether you have enriched their lives or diminished them? Isn't that the ultimate feedback you really want to know?

To ensure that you and your organization know what your

clients or customers think about your performance, you must ask them. The following tool is the best I have found for asking well and getting actionable information in return. Net Promoter Score is where mission meets math. After all, a mission without a measurement, without an accurate gauge of success or failure, is just hot air.

We covered what gets measured gets done. So if our mission is what we most want to get done, the relevant and important question is: how do we measure it? Very simply. With one question and a follow-up.

The question is, On a scale of 1 to 10, how likely would you be to recommend me, or my organization, to a colleague? Technically it is called a closed-end question because the responder rates their answer on a scale from 1 (not likely) to 10 (very likely). But then follows the critical open-ended question: What did we do to cause you to give us that score? The number the responder gives will determine into which of the three categories the customer will fall into:

- Promoter
- Passive
- Detractor

Promoters are people who respond with a nine or ten and are signaling that their lives have been enriched by their relationship with your company or organization. These people will make frequent, enthusiastic referrals for you, basically serving as unpaid salespeople for your organization. This is the kind of free advertising you want!

Passives are those who give your organization a seven or eight, got what they paid for, nothing more and nothing less. They are passively satisfied customers, not loyal ones.

They make a few referrals but are likely to be qualified and unenthusiastic referrals. They bring little energy to the company and cannot be counted on as long-term assets.

Detractors are customers who give you a rating of six or below. Their score indicates their lives have been diminished by their dealings with the company. They are not a happy crew. If one central goal of your organization is to enrich the lives of customers, these three categories are a measure of how well you are doing.

Promoters Represent Successes

Passives are just satisfied. They can't be considered successes unless the company is satisfied with satisfactory.

Detractors represent serious failures.

Net Promoter Score—where mission meets math—is a simple formula that tracks the percent of lives enriched minus the percent of lives diminished. To use this wonderful tool, commit to track results and act. I recommend asking these questions of your customers and clients at least once per year. You also can create closed-loop learning that involve customer responses to create new strategies for the organization and build these strategies into daily operations. Leadership must show by its actions that creating more promoters and fewer detractors is mission-critical.

Chapter Takeaways:

1. What gets measured reflects what is most important to

the organization. Therefore, be very intentional about what is measured. What gets measured, gets done.

2. Measurement is most effective when it is communicated, acted upon, and celebrated.

3. High-performing organizations must have ScoreBoards that indicate whether they are winning or losing and how they are progressing.

AFTERWORD

In the previous pages, I hope you have seen how simple and effective it can be to approach running an organization like a game and the engagement that results as a natural outcome. If you have worked through the exercises in this book, you have done the hard work of assembling your Playbook, which can be a useful resource to guide you in making decisions as you lead your organization. Remembering how business is like a game in terms of having an Objective, Rules, Players, Strategy, and Measurement can help you tackle the challenges and opportunities that come with leading. My hope is that the process of assembling your Playbook has been helpful in clarifying your vision and sense of direction for your organization. The finished product of your Playbook will be a useful resource to you as well, both to refer to and to use as a tool to periodically reevaluate.

Leading an organization is the best game.

I really believe that. I hope you believe it, too, and I hope you have many years ahead of fruitful, effective leadership.